Day Trading & Momentum Strategies For The Stock Market

SADANAND PUJARI

Published by SADANAND PUJARI, 2024.

Table of Contents

Copyright

Day Trading & Momentum Strategies For The Stock Market

First Edition: Jun 2024

Book Design by **SADANAND PUJARI**

About

In this Book I will discuss multiple opportunities i.e how to Day Trade Stocks, Forex, ETF & Commodities.

This Book not only discusses how to day trade but how to form a formation of day trading, Market Makers & Secrets of Day trading.

In this Book we will discuss Charts to show you how to enter and exit along with short selling.

This Book works on a variety of Day trading examples which is great for everyone. Whether you are a Student Day Trader or an Expert Day trader or learner of Stock Market.

This Day trading Book will take you to the next level, as it will increase your understanding of stocks, Forex, ETF & Gold. At the end of the Book You will be able to make your own Day trading decisions for the rest of your life.

Chapter 1

Hi guys this is cool. Future is one hour each chart. Now what's so special. Why follow this technique? The answer lies in harmony. Because basically if you follow only one indicator example MTD you will have problems as I've just shown you in the previous Book. In these chapters I showed you how some damage gives you a PI signal but you cannot make money. The reason is an example right here. Your Borchert here at work 2004 is 640 but it went down here at 12:43 90 and you are out. You never made money you lost. So the question comes up about how to solve this problem. And Dr. Drew I am bringing two indicators that are pulling a band and a CD and it from the pilothouse to Perth from the game changer because you will find many Books on the web. All usually teach you one key indicator or like two or more indicate you are following the theme line.

Now buy the same line. I mean. Example. MF PD MSEE usually follows simple stuff; it goes up and down within a certain range. Yes MSCE can go even higher but once you will experience it by looking at different stocks, different commodities, different Kapooka 90s you will learn that it's like one in a hundred times that goes beyond a certain range. Otherwise, like in many years, it moves in a certain range and that's what ISI does index for many others and who struck a strike indicator too and other indicators too. That's why they all usually follow the same trend. Now there are some indicators that work on different aspects but what I'm trying to tell you is if they're putting the same indicators the same strength indicators in one line a day doesn't help you because they are all pointing to the same line and therefore you cannot understand what to do.

In this case like pulling a band helped in that regard. It tells you that it's within the bank and within the band means that the max profit could be achieved by getting the highest point or by taking the lowest point and therefore if you are buying here as the book right right here on this day 10 what is our profit potential deal the top duction argued that exceptionally limited and there is a higher risk that it will move down. And that's what exactly happened. So it's easier for you to take risks because at the end of the day you have to understand what is happening and what is your risk on that tree. Now once the price crosses the building, your risk on the downside is limited because nine out of 10 times want to go beyond billing up and it usually follows that up.

And he did exactly that. That's the point. That's the reason to change the game plan to change the game completely. Now let me show you one more thing. It's just you know, like in missing out on the price. If I just make it big, if you look at the MSCE it makes lows on the line. Right and right here on this chart this is the first try. This is the second night. This is the third eye. This is the fourth time. So the high is like hitting your butt but this low is not breaking. Now whenever this happens this is what I call devoir between bulls and bears because you both are fighting and nobody's winning in one battle. One name was higher than this one. But then they fell off. But the brewers were not successful in getting the price to go down.

And then again the bulls ran and then the Bears won. And that's the reason you know that this is an infighting and if you look at it a price is moving up but not in a healthy sign. It's moving up but extremely painfully it's not making huge sums of money. And the reason as to fighting for further tax more MSEE crossed up once and Mythili crossed up that a buy signal. Now you're buying here at twelfth so do 140. But what suspension by the speciality is it's all really needed it stopped pulling back which means if as he's saying by then the task of emceed buying will make the price cross doubling. Now once that trust makes him cross the bridge and then a new buyer will come in those buyers who are falling to go back.

So it's like double power to poor to be buying and making sure that the price runs up feet. Now the price is not extremely drying up. It remained subdued for the next one, two , three , four , five hours. Now gone, I chose greed. Even after the market because gold is something that is straightened out around the world. So it's not that the market closes, the market creates 24 hours a day, sometimes extruding in Australia when you're sleeping in us and at other times you're trading in some other country. But it is trading 24 hours. So you can see why it's at this point it remains to be good for the next three four five hours.

Now this is like stuff that I call the hedge fund or the big investor cap. What they basically do once they know that this is a short trade they just jump in and buy themselves. You don't let the price rise. To make sure that they hold on to the price. An indication they buy. So basically they are buying everything because they know not everyone is buying it and then they certainly try and get the price up to 12 74. Now this is close to a seven day 170. This is two dogs up and it moves up up up and now it's not moving up. It's going straight and now it's moving up again straight and moving up again. But the thing to note now here is the sell side story here on this day 12:32. Now like me Marketo delegates to Yep.

Right. So you wanted to hear and so like right here so basically Engberg here. And the day ended. Sorry they Yep it ended here on this late day at this hour. So if you were bothered you would have sold it all right here. And the next day I would have the book again. Now you might ask me that. Why now? Basically to explain the Vaj I need to explain what is really happening here. The first thing is Krane. Now the crane never looks set when the market is going off. But as a day trader you will have to know when the market is switching off. So you will have to remember what to do in that case because mostly a day or so ago someone who doesn't like to keep the stock in his account at the end of the day he's basically trying to trade with Ben the day to make money and lose money whatever.

But the trade before the close he does not mind was trading like 10 hours ago. He's not someone who wants to second trade one night. So basically the presumption is the day to day. Now it sits overnight. That's why he scored today. Great. So as a gay kid if you don't want to take over night then you will. So one hour before the night this is an hourly chart. So this is the new day. This is the only day. So on this hour or on this hour you will simply stop and get up. Now the next day aka magical You can buy up and the price runs out. Now if you remember the train doesn't know you are gay. Triggering the trend will tell you something concrete. It will tell you it's Polish right here and it's bearish on this point. So the trend doesn't know you are today. But you know you are a day trader so you get out before the close before the expiry of that day.

Now once you get out the next year always and there on the open. Reason because that's how the trading goes. But if you see an opening extremely Schopper up with a huge gap then nearing the target. The reason being I'm in this Book I'm discussing different stocks different Claypoole currencies forex commodities Dempo gold that we are discussing now. Now these are different aspects but they always tell you that money can be easily made. You look at it in this Book when they were discussing creating nice profane crimes that my trade goes into profit. An extremely short profit of three four five dollars is a big long profit of 10 15 20 30 dollars.

But basically it's always in profit. So the question comes up that the money is always left in the stock market or in the commodities market in the Forex market. So you can always make money. So violent after the trade, put Open gaps up then just sit on the sideline because if you like to sell it, it puts an icon for the day close. Yeah let's put this one on sale here. And let's presume that the market opened higher the next day when it's not a problematic trade. The reason you're still in profit and the best thing or the lifting for a day trader and the credit is that he should be in Crawford. Now if you have invested in stocks stocks are known as Blue Chip blue chip companies that give people good Pelc that have good companies that are in profit.

Those are bluechip great because you can depend on them and the same be in your trading account. U.S.-South is a company and you should have a steady Pelc you should have a profitable company. Because when you invest heavily invest in your trading account because you believe it's a good cause. It's a good company. It gets paid out. So folks like a company which always carries a good. And if you are trading all bets that end up in profit then automatically your account will increase in value and therefore your Stouffer's know that you're on the right track. So right now this is seeing a sale here. Right. But is there anything by now right here? It is saying buy because it's crossing they're building a brand on top. But the MGD isn't going to buy advice. Now the second trade is a risky trick.

Now I would jump into this risky trade reason using the simple trading plenties that could save me so I buy. But I will wait for the crossover. If it crosses down I sell. Now if you look at it further it goes up up up and moves down again. Now this is what I call the defocusing part. And if you look at it this is the first time it's higher to the second floor and it's moving now. Also it's like I can't tell time that there is something wrong. So if you're in leverage get out see it crossed on the lower side and on this day it was plus on this takes minus I'm talking about the MSCE plus minus. That is his first number. So it's a sound signal. Let me check you out right here. So you brought it here at Truglio 580 and you saw Lakehead 760. Now this is a profit not a huge profit but it's still a profit. It is still a profit.

And the thing to note as I always tell you this is just look at the date here on the bottom which shows today is 26 December. And this is 26 December so it's the same day you bought it and you get it. And once you got out. Dr. Craig and your risk is limited. You're not short of going after it. And the price falls off and the price falls off and it moves up. Now this is the second most important aspect. This red line whenever it takes support on the second line. Remember they did some good things coming up because support means someone is buying on the market. Now as an investor and as a strategist I would never recommend you to buy here. This is Luli, something that you like to read. It's tempting not to create it's something to read right here.

You would know next. It's not going down. If you have a shark toilet then this is the telltale sign that there is something definitely cute on. And that's exactly what happened. It moved up to buy signals because it's closing above the building. So you will be buying it right here. This is 27 December. So it's a new day and the price moved up and down. Now one tech move down. It's a simple sell right here on this day. Now the point is this is my country. And that's what I called at this moment when I say to you that this is great because it is not helping you to be in the same place right here once you have moved up, that mostly is not helping you. So that's a risky trade. And that's exactly what happened for the two days it went up and on the 7:56 crop and in the fifth grade dropped further down. Now you brought it here at 12 16.

Now it's down at twelve thousand eighty six. Again approximately two down. So the two dollars that you make on this trade are lost and you're straight but you're still breaking one which is the best thing because at the end of the day you should for your company your investment creating account as a company that tells you if it is on the plus or minus because if you have traded stocks then every quarter the analyst tells you that they're expecting a bullish earning or a baby shortening. And that's the first major part. If there is growth in the company or not. So if you are in minus you're losing money. That's a bad thing but if you end up flat that's not as bad as losing money.

So it's something to understand now. The next most important thing is the highest cost Loehr. See this is the first time this is the second time when it would go lower and like it's starting to come back up. But there are two highs and there are not two lows because two lows is usually considered pullback and highs is usually considered parish on day. Matthew D-Jack so Osgood as you all know that the Polish momentum is slowed. So making money will be hogging. Now the question remains in this kind of trading is not the news money because the point is that you should not lose money now to say sell. So. So. And now it's moving up. This is where I call first high first low second low but we need the crossover. And this is the crossover so you can buy again.

Now I am more bullish because all of my success is far higher than any other time so I think I can tell 92 but just focus on them is Hedy mocking. It's again turning out now I've got it at 12. Right now it's 12: 91 : 40 so it's telling me to sell the next day and it's 12:32 the next day I go out. Now you might ask why the hell did I get up now. The answer lies. Two-Minute to place by right now to tell lies on what your understanding of the market is now. Always remember if I zoom it in. This is the first clue to see the second but this low is lower than the first low. So it's not that bullish. One moves higher and one moves lower. The first high and the second act looks bearish right now. If I wanted it and they just don't then I won't remove the stock.

I wouldn't leave the commodity. I want to leave the products tree. I'll just focus on the movement. Now it is moving down right down down. Now once it moves down it is breaking this low. And therefore don't know the mocking that I told you then but it's now gone. Moving. But if you just look at it again, take support on the right side and move up. But this is what I call the diverging movement. I'm zooming out to show you people who started buying here. This is the first high. Second, I worked hard. I threw it four times lower and the highs keep on dropping, the highs keep dropping but the price keeps on appreciating. So it's like confusion. Sheedy continues calling us to tell us. Get out. Don't trust . Here is the best investment error by Kroto. It's telling us to get out. So what really is happening.

Why is it confusing us? Because this is a thing that usually I do in my cravings when I'm training and I have to sell quantities. Then I would try to create this kind of food movement. And the reason it's simple. Whenever your indicator doesn't support you are buying and selling and basically your last profitable trade and detect. What you do and can get the price of that cloud 92. So it's a $10 profit but if you take a check or one to take drugs you have not made a dime out of it. You're just flat. The market has risen $10. So the question comes up: why is it happening? Basically whenever I'm doing it my email is the creator. On the other hand because I don't know that. But I know that most hedge funds or mutual funds are technical.

So when this kind of trading happens like hell there is so much good news on gold futures the trading plan is telling the wrong picture. How is it? I'll just go and buy and they just go and buy it. And once they go and buy it that's when huge falls come and if you look at it it's again by signal indicator sees by up again right here at cowled ninety five but just look like let me make it big to high again is not a good sign. You have blogged here from ninety five aid goes up. Now it's stropping it's twelve ninety four. Forty two days. The highest point is 2094 Sony and next 510 and now excelled. Now whenever you see the first time and second I move down and it's like basically a down train I always tell as I did it right here.

TSL was not done on the exact crosscourt the crossover was. Next day I saw it on the first day but I just showed you before shooting the next day that it was up and moving down. So this dog was a cell signal. Now what is it that I am looking for? Basically I'm looking for looks pretty soon. I'm wrong. I said here I'm definitely gone. And it moves up if it moves up and crosses this high I'll jump into by. What's the problem? Basically my training plan works. So I'm always in the money. My account is always in profit so I can take that risk. But my first aim or my primary aim is to thieved the losses. Whenever you are facing this kind of a problem that the price of stock or commodities is rising but the CDC continues to train you to get out get out get out then get out.

Don't be sick in the market because basically what I just told him is some major selling and he's trying to make sure that Duprey Deronda didn't just leave his indicator and jump up to say the hell with it and he just goes on to buy. Once he goes on to buy them from me as an investor it's easier to sell because he wants to. Once the indicator comes down and I have to sell huge quantities then I simply cannot do it. So I tried to make a divergence and this is divergence and the prices go up and down. Decatur is going down. So that credos continue to come up and you have two indicators and I can easily sell it to them and once it's easy for me to sell it to them then my problems are starting to get resolved.

I have to begin with two. Don't need to worry because basically my problem is I believe the market will crash down and is being taken over by someone else who has learned nothing. As you can see their indicator continues to tell you. Now if you bought it here at 2095 60 and if I were you I would just sell it to the reason the reason is everything is starting to go down low or high. Not a good mark. The lows are starting to go lower. Again not a good knock. And if you look at it it continues to fall and now it's coming back up. But this time there is a huge difference. And dexterity for us I want to tell our audience that the lows just focus on the news. I told you this for the first floor and this was a second ago.

But I have made this thing up lie so that I can tell you because this happens with all the investors to say OK is breaking just likely down it might happen. No problem like a bike. Yes they do buy Yes and you will make this mistake. And I'm just focusing on that mistake that when you do that you don't get huge sums of money. And this is what happened. But now it's moving up again. But as I am telling you the moves are up but still the highs are not up. That's not a good sign. Now it's a crossover. So you again buy it on the cross or now the 10 that and another thing to note is that we're at the end we see the pain of going down because if you look at the base rate here was extremely sharp. But now the pace is not that sharp. Ever the polls close it tells you that when you are high it's coming up but only suggesting the gator not yourself.

Now why does a new high come up? Because as I told you if I was telling and someone else is buying, losing trust is an indicator. And just like going on to buy then eventually that hedge fund or DEBT mutual fund will understand that they are being trapped. This is what I call market psychology. Eventually that trader decks to pure which will understand that someone has told him stock, someone has sold him gold , someone has sold him to five cryptocurrency and fear. Danny starts to panic and says Oh hello I made a mistake DIAK crapping and when he understands it he puts in more resources because it's known in the hedge fund if you're crap then there are only two ways out.

You take more leverage and make the price run up and in that run up try to get out because basically by showing huge orders you make that you get investors coming and to buy. And if you look at it the pope has slowed. So it means many hedge funds and many major players have started to buy because slowing pace means someone is buying it. And again selling. But just look at it, it's broken to produce low. We bought it fair here at 97 and here it's minus. Just look at the first number right here.

So you sold it at 12 ninety seven thirty. You made a 30 percent profit which is not huge but you still ended up with a plaque. Now if you look at it from your last major Craig 12:32 it's a $14 profit. But the question to see what is happening right here is that someone is getting stuck and he tries to buy it out. But then I like the magic team now.

As I told you, the major investor if he gets stuck he brings in more buying. But in a mutual fund or a hedge fund it's not that easy to bring in more buy because you have multiple traders trading different stocks or different stuff. And money already invested is just not that easy to bring up. Now I told you that whenever the pace slows it means a second highest coming but that happens only to lose its maintenance and the high has broken. Because if you look at the highest it continues to get lower and even decide it doesn't cost that high and it breaks the previous low. Now I am telling you that it's a flat trading that is pretty you know a little bit here. You lost your daughter. Let's presume you lost 30 cents to this. Not a dollar loss. I believe you saw that.

Yikes. A few cents last but the point is understanding biggy. Now the price continues to go higher. He lost it and moved higher. And you've bought your CDs continuously going lower which tells you there is something wrong. The price is not dropping, the price is not still not dropping, still not dropping. And if you focus on it it's exactly what I told you. It's exactly what I told you to come, what else is buying it and making sure that he doesn't get crap. He's not letting the price fall off and he's not letting the price rise up and right here he would have changed the leverage to buy it out. And you know the investor will also bite at $13 one tone before I move higher. That's exactly what I told you that D.M.

a domain name and was told I understand that he had made a mistake and will buy in with more leverage. And that's work. A sell up is Excel. Nope nope just moving higher higher higher. And now it's moving lower. But just let me show you one thing: just make it big and put a horizontal line right here. On this high you're seeing it cost too high. That's exactly what the stock of Credo would have done in the fall. He would have picked up more at 11:8 and pointed out and in that cry in this rise that major investor who got stuck would have caught out and he would have made sure that someone like other major investors got stuck on something he told investors to get stuck on and just look at it. It is now moving below the blue line. Not a good sign in a bull run. It should go higher and higher.

That should not come back below the previous highs. Bad stuff. And it is coming down now you're at podiums for one and you sort Yeah this is mightest toting Codie 90. So you've made toting guards a huge 1 percent gain. But understanding is someone may it is now like now is out and some of them you're investors stuck. But now what I call a major team or it can make a gap to fall to heights by going but the third is hard to come up. It does go up but to see it fall as far as false false false and even break the law this law is broken right. The price falls off by is now going straight C and even goes the MSCE goes for the. And then the price like Karachi's down it goes below the pulling up by. So now you saw what really happened in the market.

Major player first media player execs and a second major player comes up then he understands that he's been set up so he brings in more buying so that people see that buying and debt stocks with a bang right here and a trend up to the highest point. And in that process the second major investor gets out and then the market crashes. See that's the whole thing. That's the game that when major and minor players are fighting we capture. Thank you.

Chapter 2

Hi guys, today we'll discuss the future. You know chalk. Now we all know basically what it means to day but I always tell my students to basically have a broker that charges extremely low commissions and then try to trade according to get trained because trained is your friend now. Let me show you. If you look at it alright, short selling right to 68. This is next December 7 times 7. And it fell off, fell off a loaf, fell off, fell off, fell off, timestamped eighty four point eighty five twenty six seven eight nine ten one and now seven. See right here. So basically since this is the turn on sixte KILL THIS IS SO what you have to quit a shock sell and Square-D day is complete. Then on the second shock toward him at Yeah this is the first kind of cross section fall and it's about falling falling falling and I can't what I said by 12:54 out what a complete reason because if you want then you would have died.

But basically it's saying so so you can not do anything excessively. Then again just look at it right here. You think so. Got 52 saying buy your Ikea now this is what I call the trading plan. However my presumption or assumption or plan is an important aspect. What is that? That is close to above zero. Number one. Number two is lows. Now if I just tune in today's methionine shock or look for Lowe's example right here it was making a high and low high and low. So basically selling that it was in a box so you need this low to be broken for the price to go your number one number two number to go bad.

Now it makes the most money you wanted to bring about on the downside and go slower, take breaks on the downside and goes slower not that the blink of an example it said by right here you would have bought at 68 back on the south take note you would have sold that same 2068. It's nothing. Why? Because the price is within the blink of an eye. And that's not a good move. Now let's discuss it for you now. The reason I'm switching to buy now is because if I just zoom out now, this is a 30 minute Chalk Talk, which means it's extremely long term for things to change and how the matches just close. This is a high low dose of the high dose the lows are getting higher to tell him it's a good mark to buy number one. Number two now it's turning back upright.

So we'll wait for the cross when it does cross try to see the first number is Plus right here. Plus it means by the way I have it like Shaktar or scraped out. Now have you bought at Best 40 to 70 and for about 70 cents and the price moved up. It's moving up now. Trading head on trust. December 1:30 p.m. the price is moving higher and Great Lakes Crossing on the other side. Now is the time around here. Is 9 p.m. so you'll know that the trailing will stop and that you can take your body at 40 to 45. That's a $10 profit. You'll make it and you run away. Now remember this is the chalk chalk you're making. This kind of profit is $5 $10 $15 not Baker. Now Vinicio is not popular there.

I like the franking creating some time or pain that makes the profit bigger and smarter. But take $5. What I'm trying to say is pulling a back seat. The price is going to be in the building and not outside. So what profit margins will be used is not being able to make money. And before you will have a problem. But let me show you the next feature that I will tell you about. Wait now on it up now. Now I guess what is on the CD. So if I would have been shocked , sort of like say here on the set of building a bank, breaking it is 2044 right. It is. Twelve forty four point forty four dollars per cent the price goes lower and jumps back up my lower comes back up goes lower comes back up and opens higher. Now we trade it. Let me check. I am strong.

I can wait a minute please. Yeah right who. I called 40 for 50. Went like and this is. Don't. This is 13 13. And I need to open higher. But it's high and close to above, troubling back what you want to know by again. Now what did you learn here? Ulang Let me zoom out and show you that the loans were getting higher and he was shocked at selling it. Now I have done the structural test to show you I should go back to school and go back and continue to go to bed. This last point was 12:30 12 for forty three to 40 to 60. For us a fall. But it was a problem that kept on getting higher. And if I just want to show them the highs this high is lower in this high higher and now this high even further higher so it is also important never shut off once the lows are getting higher.

But when you. Now if you read back right to let me show you. Wait a minute 47. I destroyed the building of bangs. So I made only eight bodyguards. But what you have observed right now at 46 90 our profits would have increased for the and rightly so. So 12:56 12:46 12:56 that's a $10 profit. And that's huge. It's exceptional. It's awesome. And Antos crossing the high now taking note as I always tell you the highest point on the MSEE is if I pay this highest point that's back and make a green line for you to see and we zoom in to the current flow you see that it crossed the current level. So it's telling us that MECC is currently trading at the highest point and conflict can go flip and that's exactly what is happening now. It is making a first time and the second time and moving lower now I always recommend my students to only buy because buying is mostly the most easiest to read and for the most like what I call the sweet trade dudes in Cleveland is now let's check for the moves up up and now it's moving down down down. Now a cell signal right here.

See. Now what can you do? You can't do anything you need to accept this last part. There is a learning curve here. What is that? That is that if the price moved beyond the building ban then it is a higher level. But if it stays in the building U-Bahn then there is a lot of work out. So if you've seen a PI or a cell you need a place to cross above it. Otherwise you can just place a stop loss example if you bought here at 12:56 90 then simply you are Karplus would have been 12:56 40 right here on the low of this cattle. If it hits that you were out the season because you already know that if the price crosses up after building about Danny to polish you Vampa it's crossing upright here right. This is 0.00 eight like me and I can for you yeah right here it's 12:56 by right.

But you and I know that once it crosses 12:58 then it will be zooming out but we will always like to shrink by region because these two guys are all too important. And you might ask how that is what I call the super calculation super calculation. What really happens is if the price goes from $2 to $3 That's a 50 percent gain. And it grows from 5:42. That's a 100 percent gain. Now just focus on it from Bill Titos. It's a 50 percent gain. And from 10 to $6 it's a 100 percent gain back from six hundred to six dollars. It's 300 percent the 200. To just look at it. On the flip side it says 50-100 percent. So in total time 50 percent back from bluegill takes it Sturrock put in gay to the same be from 12:56. Both 12:57 that's a small lever done. But from this I will tell the highest closing it's an exception.

Let's check what happens. It doesn't go up and it stays down. See now it has been like breaking the deadline then you should simply say if I were you and the price went up. That's the point. And now it's coming back down and breaking the line. I will get out. Why are you scared? You bought your 12:56. This is closer to 640. Get out it moves up and down. Now it's what they called Good morning. Now this is what I call the flip side from where it was going up. Just look at it. Boom gap up and now it's going up. It fell off and right Kerick told us to sell 12:58 the boxer felt. It's a 50 cent gain. In between these two like light now the concept is understanding the trade. Why don't you have fifty eight when you start this kind of a good Kincannon.

Then you stop loss should be on the lowest of that Kincannon army remember to serve God your profit. If the price falls then you should have got it right here on the low. Get out. And the second most important thing is you're trading day trading. So anyway on the day you believe you have made good money out but don't get me into unless and until the MSCE crosses down an example here and then it crosses up a cake. Then on the upside by a game like you remember save got profit and get out whenever you believe you have made enough money for that day. The reason is we are trading day trading and day trading is extremely fast trade and making money is problematic like a teen because basically the problematic stuff is the broker he charges you so much that it's exceptionally hard to carry.

And so the solution is understanding the game. Now if you bought it at 12:58 or did you buy it. I remember you brought it here. Yep I can, it should be here. Yeah. So Sixto Denslow off 12:16 that's it all again right back on the highest point. We'll talk to you. That's what a doggie takes in a day, so be vigilant. Or you can simply place a stop loss and stop loss from the lower level. The reason why it is good is because I play the game with extreme risk. If you believe you have made good money out because at the end of the day I don't. Later I paint a trader who is not buying gold. He's simply not buying gold. He's simply diluting the price. He doesn't care if it goes to a hundred thousand pounds or a hundred dollars per ounce today. That doesn't count them, he doesn't care if the gold supply is increasing or the gold price or whatever.

He doesn't care what his aim is to make that count. And if you're trading 30 minutes that's an extremely short virgin. So you have to get in and get out extremely sharp. You have to understand you cannot sit down for the whole day. You have to make the trade accordingly. And the solution. Understanding the trend. If you believe you have made huge sums of money from 12:56 do glove 60 TDX huge gap. Why say take so I always tell my students what learning and training is. Not for students who are longer because in the longer run if you can hold onto the stock or commodity for that Nike or Nike and you can stay put. Then they don't have a problem. They can eat for their higher profits. In my day, I've shown a huge profit of hundreds of percent.

But the concept in decorating genius completely in not much trading you are looking at what the company does and all that stuff. But in day trading that doesn't count every kind of research goes out of the window. The only name is look at the key. My near one day your name, your game, your plan and your like everything is aimed at that day. You don't care what the stock market is because your aim is only on that day and that's how it is. If you bought here you would be selling here. The reason is simple. Now show me one more thing. Now you are not happy to like Peg the trade for the next day. They are like two sorts of traders, one who can go for the next few days.

So they and Caig are ready for our longer term chart for our leader Max Jack for that. But there are other credos who don't trade overnight who don't keep their trade overnight. So if you bought into the game plan, aim right. Right. So they sell right here on the next day you would have, say, bought a Gulf of cake. The price moved up once you saw a profit of six seven eight dollars. You cannot sit there and get your profits in your pocket and close to the terminal close to software. Reason because at the end of the day we all know that profit margins are limited on the day trading level. If that didn't get out don't take on it too.

Chapter 3

Today we will discuss the future. But on the fly. Manic Jock these days is what I call fixed . It's not what I call a normal Posten trading. It's xtreme tree. It's extremely fast. So you were the creator. If you jump into it you can jump out. It's something that is like really fast and the basic theme of that creation is to understand daddies to understand that you cannot flip between buy and ShoreTel. We didn't see De because the training is so fast you have to have a presumption of what the next 10 days will be. Then you paid either by or shock so what you trade only what you get are great but it's extremely fast. Now if I just zoom in and show you. It works on the same level but just look at the highs. This is the first time this is the second time now in the previous one hour chapter I told you how.

From the second I found out but if someone means you are stuck he'll try to play and bring it back to the high C it brings to the Torah and then it dropped off and I just left. I don't know if I can get that much data because five minutes of data is something that is extremely limited. But the point is even with that limited data base point is the lowest point in so many hundreds of cons.. There will be a proximity of a thousand kinds of right who are 500 to 700 Counter-Strike and you have not seen such a fall. Now such a file is like it's many years old to break because it's basically telling you okay don't worry that is the major fault. Because often the default The market usually dries up and if you look at it the price rose hair back up and is now crossing the previous high.

So it's a poor rock and the price if you look at it is going up, but just focus on the price. It's now not crossing the building on top which is not a good thing. It should but it's not falling off. So it is linked back back and right here it has crossed saying goodbye to here 13:34. And just look it was up and now it's again going straight and now it's so. So you would have me for four dollars because it's a five minute break. So even a team for its profit is great because it's just five minutes away. And as I've already told you and I've worked in all my quarters to go to the level of creating the high the profit the shock the level of creating example that has five minutes. So don't expect a 100 dollar gain in that like shot, don't always expect smaller and smaller and smaller again. Now why am I discussing five only checks because one student asked me what it took to take five minutes.

So I wanted to show them that five make shoots. What does foster 46 shops? So if you're creating 5 and it's like you are sitting in a locked room with no one can enter and no one can ask you anything because the moment they ask you anything and you try to explain them up then your focus is removed from the market and it takes 20-30 minutes to get back. They get focus to get the focus back to the market. And that is like changing the game. Just look at it now it's crossing up again. So it's a buy signal. And now you presume you know about it here. Your focus was to have moved and you couldn't focus it and it went up at the crossing.

Now if you look at it the price is not going anywhere but the MSCE is not even crossing on the lower side which makes it look like a buying machine because at the end of the day when you're in the news to see what really happens down as the prices go bad. So our profit expectation is already lower. We are not expecting a good profit margin because of good graphics I mean. The price crossed doubling back on top stock. So you are sitting on the sidelines and now it is crossing on the top side the ET we've moved up and now it's a game moving straight. Now you remember on the five minute shock it room straight many many times it wasn't like making you a mad person because this kind of thing happens a lot.

Now this is turning 30 for 30. And this buy is turning 30 472 you lost 40 cents. Now on the fiver each after a five minute stock you lose money lock Tony 30 cents will come a lot. So if you're considering five hours trading then accept this problem because basically I'm a five minute chart in a day. You might trade for five times a day max. What I'm talking about is the max on an hourly chart. The average is around one or two trades in a day. If you move Cutrone much the average will go to tame folks rates. But if you want to find where the average averages that they will move from like 30 to 50 crates in a day. Why? Because it moves a lot and after Kotok it says sell right here. But just look at it after a few five minutes it will say buy again right here right here saying buy again see it's a plus sign.

So we'll be buying again. Now you just made I think last and I were buying two boards higher because that's how my cookbooks and now exclusively now again you have lost money. But this is how the five minute droid goes. See it's the cell now. This is the thing to note this time. Second, a second is exactly the same as the first time. And just now dropping my name which makes you high is bad. It means it will drop badly.

28

It goes straight straight and doesn't fall off. Now it's moving up again. Now what will I do? I was thinking it's going down but doesn't it swing by again. And I have to buy again because if I am Polish then I will buy again. And why am I bullish? Because the malls are starting to get up in your and the highs are getting lower.

Now the lows are getting higher. I don't follow any signals from the five minutes Jack. I mean my father from a long chalk because five weeks is something that I call a bit more gambling because basically you have no idea what's happening. And the cold is all over the place. Now just look at it, you're buying it again here and you're selling it again here. Now for a short period of time you have forgotten one Craig Croyde and two Twiggs and you have not made money in any one of them. The reason it's in a box and I know that market is already doing. And if you look at it the highs are not keeping out the highs are getting lower. So I told you that currently if you were bullish then it's not a market for you. It's not moving in your favor. Now actually gained by.

But if you look at it, it's not even crossing the highest high in the bank. So it's good. Not a good market to you because basically to buy. You need to press to cross to higher moving about now except my hair taking time to sound. But if you move like you're on it no cost about putting a bandage within the like pulling the band which is not a good sign. And then you are up in the band that Dan does like crap and you are flattered. It's mind replied. You can lose more money when the price is within the bowling and then out of it because basically all the cases are designed to help you make money. Now you make money when the price goes from totally let's say 40.

That's the sound of our profit in it and in going on let's say $5 profit from there we're still not. Bad if the price moves within let's say 32 Tony to me and it's only a $2 gain. And within that $2 again your profit margin is only a dollar because basically the signal will come a bit late. So in that lateness you will lose the profit. But as your profit margins start to decrease, decrease , then it starts to eat in your pocket and that's. On the five. This is the problem because the trading range is reduced. Now I just looked at it from just a range of billing about 13:34 and Baulkham is Todi 32. But again just blogging and going again I need to make money. It's exceptionally hard because basically the signal is a bit late.

So you could not make $2. You can expect that you can open the door. So you are earning 30 -50 cents. That's the problem. And therefore finally Sharks have a huge problem because the gap between the two candidates is extremely limited. And you cannot free trade because you are in a limited risk plonk. You brought it here at Todi and took it to 70 and sold it here at 30 -30 -40 cents a day. Now you may ask , "What's the profit in it?" The profit is in the making. Now I am still searching for the movement but once I find it I don't show you how fast it can make your money because a five minute trading is known to be the extreme shop moment. It's something that is exceptionally higher in a five minute chart. Your losses will always range within 30-50 Cent but your profits will be far higher. You know profit will make you like a King.

Now it's moving up again. So you have black data again here. Right. And just look at it move higher and higher. Now if you remember we were losing what we wrote using 2056 And if you look at it we bought it here at thirteen thirty two forty six and we sold it here at 13:34 40000 that took our game back the highest point was the highest point was. Let me check. Twenty five. It makes a ten dollar profit. So that $10 profit was ten times the return of the losses. If you were losing 30 cents then now in this case you would have earned ten times more than your loss. Now this is a profit like gun that last investor into a five minute job. But the point is how many trades are profitable in it.

One trade lasted two three four five five losses and one good only one got one good trade was so great that it gave Obek 10 times to get done. So your five kids would have got absorbed by the First World Trade and it would have given you more profit than the Dec. 1 trade. So this is how you understand what really is happening because basically the understanding of five minutes is that it gets an exceptionally profitable trade in terms of losses. I'm not talking about a physical like profit, the physical profit is still one to two dollars. It's going to exceed that. But the point is it's far higher in terms of losses. But as we have seen there are so many trades and you have to be exact to the second to buy.

You cannot hold it and wait but even if you are at the exact second all I don't believe no one can be at the exact point at the exact day and human nature is it takes times like I understand it. So finding a job is something beyond human. But if you're telling it to anyone remember you have to keep on losing losing

losing to find that one good trait because that one trade will change everything. Now when Emma the five cast makes a Double-O and moves up then you will see your light go days have started. And when good news starts then you are profitable trades will always be like hire now right here. You're buying a peek at let me show you. Yeah. 13:34 90 and what happens next the price goes straight straight moves up straight.

And it's so nobody here. Yeah. Thirteen thirty five. Ken and Michelle 13:34 90 percent say it was. So now again you lost 20 cents and you have cracked a bad thing. That is the highest highs are again getting lower. So it's again telling you that the good news might be bad. Just look at it. It went to our room and the next day it went higher again. So now that's what I call a human video in five minutes of being British. You would need to jump up to buy up for five minutes. Right. And within five minutes you would have to buy it again at 13:26 44. And a higher price moves up up up and now it fell reboarded to here at thirteen thirty six forty. And we would have sorted at last check 1.0 we sent again. You'll make money. Brilliant money $1 30 cents. Brilliant.

Europe re-activated orders are 20 -40 -50 cents but now it's a billion profit. But the Kuwaiti savings how can you sell and within five weeks buy it out again. the problem. That's the real game. That is the golden secret of five minutes straight. But it does work. And the reason as I've just told you is the profit margin is so huge that you won't find this kind of profit margin anywhere else. It's pure gambling. Reason being it's fastness, it's so fast that if you can trade it then it will always give you a profit because my trading plan is so good.

But at the end of the day if you somehow missed it you can buy it on the slopes you have to bite on disclose that team trade would become a flat rate because this is toting Todi seven Tony and this is 30 days and 70 Fortuny 40 cent Barford and that 40 cent profit minus the previous losses would be a flat trade. So you never made any money so you cannot miss it. You have to be an exact day, Ben. You can say that you aren't tempted. I divide it exceptionally hard. But as I just told you a golden rule. It made a little for you Mike Double-O and now it's making higher highs. When it wasn't looking higher highs and dropping that was not a good sign. Now it is a good moment. And if you move further out it says sell but whenever it from Moscow

buy again then that would be a good profit. Just look at it right. Had crossed the blink of an eye I would have bought it at 13:28 50 and it would have moved higher. At one moment in time I would have me taking 40-50. Our profit. HUGE profit. But then the sell off would have been 13 thirty nine twenty. So it's just $1 cents but it's still higher than our last word Kate. Got lost in 30-50 cents. So you can see it worked. But you need to be exceptionally late into the market. You can sit on the sideline and tank on your trading 500 claiming is a no brainer creating It's simply following the crank. Simply following you on the cake no matter what.

Chapter 4

What is long put out this is a really important chapter because it will really change your outlook. Two words short selling now Lockport is in itself an option strategy. Longboarding gives you the right but not the obligation to Shockoe. What does this lake Koch mean? It means that once you buy a long put when you put kids along then you have no problem saying too short. What does it mean? It means that if you are an owner of a long put down it means that if you like then at any time in an American option you can go and clean that option. That is you can set it off to give you shock told shows at a specific price. Let's say that the price is $40.

You walk along put the price fell to 20 dollars on 20 dollars you can simply claimed all along that you have already purchased and asked the seller of too long put to short sell you shares at dollar forty price so therefore he will be like giving you shirts minus 1000 shirts short or 40 dollars. At today's prices of $20 you can simply get shares from him and sell them on the market. You simply made $20 profit at that point. Number one. Number two with whom your shorts operate at $40. But the market went to $60. You were wrong. But in Lamport you have the right to claim the option but not the obligation. Which means you can simply like the option to expire. If it is 30 days. Why would you wait till 30 a day and then let it expire?

The loss is only the premium paid upfront. Either you are in profit or in loss in both cases the premium paid up front is gone and therefore the short selling makes complete sense to you because if the market falls it is a money making machine because you have no risk and only your profit and in an American option you can claim that at any time at any time you like. If the price falls Still let's say from 40 8 for security you can simply claim that the price can go to Canada and come back to Todi as well. But once you claim it and like to sell it on the market it's gone as simple as that. The best part now you put you into a long put on the file and basically due to the late fall in value of option increases.

So you are going to like earning in that sense because once you think about it, let's see what you mean by the option and have that option. I'll do it. Just describe the options you want to own in that sense. Now it can also be used as a hedge against a long position. Now what does this mean? It means less to you. I am owning a thousand shares at $20 and I believe it will go two hundred dollars. The price is right just below 40 and now I believe from 40 it can fall to 2005 and then come back up. So to save myself I simply chalk sell I like potatoes along but which acts as a shock sell position. Or did you want to talk to you? And if I like to buy and import, it gives me the right but not the obligation. So I know that if the market falls from say 40 back to Kuini then what will I do?

I would simply keep those options and sell my shoes at the top at 40. Now we all could be wrong. And before long put is the best hedge against a long position because you have the right to sell right at the top where you park the port and the price lower after that. No risk at all. And you can simply say so on top and buy again at the bottom because you already publish on the long term strategy so you get the best of both worlds. If the option is exercised early or expires in the money then you're being a shock self-pleasuring. Now it means that if you claim Let's say that you are really only an option and you exercise that then at that point your account will be holding minus one thousand shares which is like basically shortcutting same thing or if it expires after 15 days on its expiry date then when you are Kancheli be credited with minus one thousand.

So basically it is a short selling position but till the time you don't like exercise it can't won't minus 1000 chips or minus a hundred shares. It will only show you a long part which doesn't give you any losses because keeping them big is the max loss on long put is the best to you for shockingly Nick. Kate Short selling comes with unlimited risk because if I shock short today then I know if the price moves beyond my buying beyond my short selling price then I'm already lost. But in the long part that's not the case and stock can rise above your selling price and continue rising in your long part.

You want to lose a dime more than the premium paid. Whereas in a naked short selling it's a lot as Whereas long put offers with the same benefit. Exactly the same benefit without any additional risk or without even the risk associated with naked short selling. The only risk is the premium paid as a long put that the max risk cannot exceed that and options come with increased liquidity. Now you might see some shares, some stock that comes with really small liquidity. You cannot shock sell it. Let's say there are three hundred thousand shares traded in the day.

So if you are shocked, you sold 30000 shares. Boom you're gone because you're selling 10 percent of the total daily volume. That's huge. But like options usually you need liquid stock options to be trading at higher volume. Therefore you have a high chance of squaring a cap whereas the only difference between options and short selling is to compete because the options you are paying a premium. In short selling you're not paying a premium. That's the difference. But if you look at the risk then all the risk could fall into options category. It's something of the past like stuff that there is to offer in shock selling. So that's what it is. Thank you.

Chapter 5

Hi guys to play your list because PowerShares coo coo coo trust Dallas sees one. And it's a one hour chalk. Now you might ask why I have chosen this ETF as the reason behind it. The reason is it gets EGFR lows. The Nasdaq index. So basically you're getting your power from the Nasdaq index now, almost all choose the ETF that offers the highest power and as Vinu Nasdaq offers the best return over the past many years. So it makes NASDAQ one of the best ETF because Nasdaq rises almost like it contains the best tech companies. So automatically the ETF will be owning those companies and as their stock price rises so will the ETF price to basically your owning a hedge fund yourself.

And by creating Index ETF you're basically improving all the falls and getting all the rights. So your aim is to get the most price now as you can see right here. It's falling falling falling and the price ultimately went Cloward then ditch building again and then here as they quickly go and there is value when you're on the toilet and it never really crossed up. It went down, down and down. So it makes us believe in the king that he liked longest and in the making. Zoom out and I make it big. So this fall if you look at it it's reaching the extreme lows. For the extreme close one but this low and this low doesn't offer extreme like in French.

It's different and currently the Damascene is falling further down. So it tells us that it may be the king that low any time. And as you can see I've just zoomed in and it has fallen for the next three days. Now if I just point my mouse here or if I just make a line I heard online on the news two of these two nos. You'll see that it is going further down back and it goes further down. It could present a change in trains, maybe coming sooner than we thought because this is what we'll do when a road crosses extreme highs or when it falls to extreme lows. A change in trend usually happens. Now a change in trend doesn't mean that the price will go to new highs.

What it means is the first target is the top billing a band but usually doubling up on contract. So the price of the toppling of dangler starts to fall and so will your target price and goes across a doubling of and then you can expect previous highs to be reached. And one teaches that. And the third attempt is to make new highs. So that's how the game plays. Now executing that risk bottoms off MSCE. So you're expecting me to pull on coming around the corner. And right there it's a crossover. So you buy now as you can see before the crash away opening higher. Now many of my students ask what this opening means.

Let me tell you now what really happened is like 80 percent of the retail investors don't follow a strategy. They just look at the chart. Sorry not to chart but they just look at the ticker. That is the price movement and they decide according to the price movement. Now when the price moves with such a gap it opens higher then the people suddenly get confused. People were shocked that they came to buy the people who didn't know anything. They believe more buying is coming today. So basically it's like a play when you bring everyone into the buying Argin. And this is how the changing trend happens because everyone is buying so they don't have any idea of what's happening.

And if you look at it they keep on opening it higher so there are more and more people who rush into it and eventually it crosses the bank right. Now it means a good bull run is coming. And the high point may be like it's within our reach. It's easier. It falls off. Now just focus on the Quantic closed higher. Now the bigger player will be moving in because now they believe it's like making a good price index or a good stock or whatever you can say. But it represents a great pulling signal. So what they do is we'll put it to work right here for the opening higher opening higher. So it would like bringing people to buy. It's opening the door to basically telling people to get off the train. How could somebody with this kind of a gap. People panic.

And this panic brings selling because certainly to see prices go lower and that's not a good sign. You panic sell and a big player buys from them now right here is the crossover. Right. So you sell it right. Right. And it's a profitable trade. Now the question comes up how much profit gives me a break. Let's check. Now let's check the buying rate was 142 11 minus the selling rate was 145 50. So you made it to go on a nice set within just a macro a few hours although it took many days because it's an hourly canon so it usually lasts for many days. So now the question comes up as a daytrader how to get out. Because basically you made money but you need to get out. And how do you do that?

You get out here next year to open fire so you'll be losing money then comes the minute you have then come here the next day it opens lower. So what you lost here 50 or 60 percent is regained here then comes recommend a minute then comes here again the next Jadavpur opens entirely And then comes here and then before the next day you sort it out. So now if you check it out the total gain that he made was to go to 29 cents. OK. Now let's check it close here at one point seventeen and open at 140 293. So that's 20 70 76 cent 0.7 6 7 6 plus sorry minus here. Object 1:44 46 and opened at 144 10. That's a $26 gain for us. So the top two like LOFFLER means 40 cents right here closed at 144 41 and open at 144 So 20. So that's a $30 loss.

That's a fairly decent loss. Hey it's 145 45. And the next day it opened at 1:45. 68 so that's 20 cents loss. One two three. So in total we lost a dollar. Let's presume we lost a dollar in total, maybe to go take nine. Thanks. So at the end of the day at the end of the trade we may still make $1 or 40 cents now although it doesn't look so much correct but it is great because if you're creating a Todman church done one of 40 sank like a thousand words it's a fourteen hundred Donaghey That's huge. The reason it's a smaller quake is you are trading it for the ballgown you aren't sitting here for like $100 gain in a shorter period.

You already knew that. You have to buy and sell the next to a lake before the close to buy the next open buy to sell it and to buy and next day on the open to you just did that. And currently we are not analyzing that within the first minute what the movement is because in the past five minutes. There is a movement which can be like Good for you your losses could be good for them but even if we don't think like that you're still seeing that even on the shortest turn of an hourly chart you're making money because at the end of the day it's about money it's not about how much money you make but it's about if you're making money or not. Because if you look around 90 percent of the day traders would tell you they don't make money.

Why do they don't make money? My plan even though it's extended to many many days it's like one day to day three day day. And on the fifth day we crossed it. So it extended to a week but we still ended in profit even though we had the risk of opening lower off like selling lower. And next year's Open is higher. Even with that risk we ended up in Crawford. So this means we're doing something correctly. It means we were on the correct pot even though it was an hourly trade. If you ask a swing trader then he won't. He will say that's the most dangerous part. But we still made money. If we go further it goes straight up. But if he's not saying by now it's going flat. But on this day you open and close above the building to go back to. A bull ran for us.

You'll buy it here. And what. What. Six forty nine. And the crossover happens the next day and the price goes up. And let's check with something that is now there isn't a cell signal. But what really happens week a minute oh OK this is the day close connected Open's floor. So you made money because you closed on Tequila's you thought it higher. And the next day open it lower so you block lower right too. This is the dazing you sold but it opened higher. So on the next beta you never made anything special. But as it went straight let me show you. If you look at the top number it was all positive for the 0.2 little point it was 6 9. They opened you know once then it suddenly jumps up 0.5. And this is the cell signal right here on this red counter.

So you simply choose a cell single. Right. So when you bought it you bought it at 146 forty nine. So let's try to get 146 49. Sorry I've got 146. Forty nine. And we sold it here at 147 Tony minus 147 Saudi. So we made a dollar and 21 cents. However, our trade bank for one day today. And on the Tour de squared. So our risk was only right. It closed at one point down 46 and opened at 146 97. That's what 50 cents gained for us. And I could close at 140 phone text text and I opened at 147 86. So that's the 23rd off that huge I think it goes from 46 to 50 Cent and X 66 and that's 20 cent lost and you gain 30 percent. So that's not going to anyone that's one 151 so you'll make a door and 51st engaged. And if you have a thousand she had that fifteen hundred dollar profit again. So you're making money. Why not?

You just need to see it on the whole that's. Did you do anything extra? No. You only waited for it. You only saw what it was doing and it. Perfect. You never had to see anything special wrong. Just look at it. I'm showing your trade that made you a 20 percent gain on selling on the night and buying on the day. That's it. So basically at the end of the day you gained a $1 50 cent profit without doing anything special. Awesome is if we move further it falls falls falls falls falls but it stays within the bill and goes back which tells us that we can again make money as and when the crossover happened. And that's the crossover. One hundred and forty eight dollars a year for St. body to and the price moves up up up and that's a sales signal is this a sell. No this is a sale.

So you sold him. Now you made approximately 1.40 S. here and 1.50 here and walked off here. It's 140 years to do a full so 1:48 to. Minus the selling price 140 so it's only showing 147 Tony selling. That's a 27 cent loss, nothing extraordinary. Nothing at all. And the best thing we forgot. Now this is closing time. You cannot buy here you have to buy the next day on a very open floor at 147 81 and sold at 147 77. That's only a T.S. loss. And that's only a day trade. So three cents off is nothing. As you're making $1 a 40 cents profit here and $1 50 cent profit. So he said at last. It's not even countable and it again jumps back up. Right here you'll be buying again at $1 48 cents is it here or here. Here $1 $148 and 39 cents. Hundred forty eight thirty nine.

And the price goes straight straight straight comes up straight straight straight. Now whenever you are straight as the day trader were to you to be vigilant and get up early. Now here we boarded at 148 Tony 9 and told it at 148 34. So that's a five cent trough the next day open rewarded 848 so windy and would have soared to Yep right here. So we bought it to turn green and 48-70. And so were eight hundred and forty at sixty nine. That sets you off. So if you are looking at eight you've made for great too profitable great awful one dollar and 50 Cent here and 1.40 Thank you. And this was what a 50 cent loss was, this was what a 1 cent loss. So if you're looking at it you're losing that thing your profits are extremely high and your losses are an insect.

And that's what makes you a good day trader because at the end of the day you are in profit. And as I'm showing you if you can sell on the clothes and buy next day on the open that's not even bad because at the end of the day you're still making the crude and flat write it the last great because the nonprofit grade it doesn't matter because you're still getting $1 50 cent profit. So the gaps don't matter because they will automatically be filled within the profit. Right. Now we made a 20 cent profit in the gap. And right here on 19st in within the gaps on the open close. But even with those gaps we never lost money. Only five percent . So that's what the game plan is. You have to understand this is how a daytrader can work even on the longer run.

He can sell all night and buy the next deal on opening that to Andrew. If I look at the current view of me for trade and made nothing on the last two trades on the first two trades we made a good profit of approximately $2 and right here again a buy signal sees crossover happening. You'll be buying Iodo getting to know it openly and going below the building of and that's never a good sign. So if you're buying you're being vigilant. The price moves straight straight straight and says sell your IQ. Now reboarded here at 1:48 takes you on this sell he too many sell is 1:48 thoughtful 1:48 Texas. That's a 30 cent loss. If you're looking at it, the losses are extremely fixed. We aren't losing money this close is 1:48 71.

This is 149 to that 20 cent loss here as well on the open close. So that's a 60 cent loss. But the thing to note as I'm repeating again and again is your losses are only in cents. This is the max. Like the biggest loss of 60 percent but your profits are like double or triple digit $1 50 Cent 1.40 think Dr. knockback. Now it continues to fall and you wait. Now it's a crossover thing again. So that's what my point of view is. The thing is when it goes polluted willingly the rising power decreases unless and until it goes up. And that's what I wanted to show you right here. It did go lower but once it went higher here you had a higher chance to make money.

Then he drank flat. So he lost money lost money lost money and then it opened the door. You lost 60 you think. But the point is you gained $2 90 Saint-Cyr and 60 Santerre and 565 68 approximately 70 sacks were lost. So you still managed to get to decent gain within all the street that sparked the long run as. But if you look at it right here this was the first time this was the second. So you knew that the crane was down. And that's exactly what the price is doing once it touches the blue line again you'll have a higher moneymaking chance again. This is the number one thing. Number two it went up for specific ratings. Now what do I mean by that. I mean once you see any stock falling off to extreme lows you can buy to make a small gain and then you can back off and look for some new stock. This is a striking new take on it.

Chapter 6

How gays today we will discuss PowerShares QQQ ETF on the theme there Chuck. Now it's extremely smart. So it offers higher creating opportunities. However the perfect number will also be reduced. So you have to be vigilant in that term. And the last figure it ought to be used it's like smaller training with smaller profits. Now the thing to note. Please please please remember this. David untimed When will happen your budget here at 1:54 12:4 and the next day it opened higher and vented or. Now that is like lighting. I need to inform you guys slightly about what to do now. Always remember if you're bored too within the next 30 minutes it rises and gives you a few cents. Then the next open you would never buy. Please don't buy it now. I know in the previous chapters I've told you to buy clothes and buy on the open.

I have but it certainly limits. There are certain rules that are cruel if you're buying it then doubling up and then you have a range trading. You cannot expect the price to go above tippling so the price will stay within that range. It cannot exceed just that. So if you bought it if you bought it here and the next day it made you a few cents from what you had before thirty five to one for fifty four forty nine to 15 cent profit. OK but if you are buying at the top which is not doubling about that don't you think any profit making opportunity for you. Yes it can go above and beyond doubling again. Yes it is. But you have to look at the risk reward ratio. There is a high risk buying here and that's exactly what happened at 24. And by the time it said Sell you would have lost X-Gene money.

This is 1:54 wonder 48. And this is 1:53 20:27 Dax walk to the door and 27 cents. That's a huge loss. Huge to remember this. This is the kind of opportunity for you to buy and sell clothes on the next day or open. You are willing to buy but not that high. So do check it out where it's opening now in the pink slip chapter on the one hour chart on QQQ. I discussed you buying but the drop like stock had already gone beyond doubling back. So you were already like going up in the UP movement. You can sell on the Lower Lakes, sell under clothes and buy on the open. That makes sense but it's not crossing double. So your profit once you were buying your profit margin was still here.

Unless and until it costs double go back. But before that you have your profits right. Except on the toppling of an open at such a higher rate than docked not your money making machine. That means it's not. Don't risk it. So does this kind of situation where you have to stop your hand from buying the stock. You have to stay away. You have to understand that there are sometimes they're you ignore that are like buying signals. And if you ignore it then you don't buy it unless and until it closes above the pulling of that. Now the second scenario is here. You bought it here. No. Hero $154 six. It went higher for the next 30 min and then fell off. Fell off and right here et cetera. Once you do 88 this is 154 06.

That's $1 or 20 cents. Yes. This is a kind of loss that the plan cannot. Let me give you a way out. However, the way out could be fun by yourself. Now how do you form that? You bought it on the heels of this candor. Right it went higher and B-24. Now whenever things are not going Aspel your plan then you should have a stop loss plan. Now please remember that Dinda of mine as we have discussed earlier is a higher loss making chance than once the price crosses the building of an undertow. So you can limit your losses by putting a stop loss on that kind of over your back or on the previous low care. If this low kind of lives outside the building go onshore it's not really making sense to put a fear but this or this can and it will limit your losses to extreme points.

Example you bought here at 154. There were six. The low here is one fifty fifty seven. That means a 50 cent loss if you would have put it here. That would have meant a 45 cent loss. So the concept is to understand what's happening if things go bad then you have a TINC to go and get out. However once you are I hope they don't buy distressed rates. Either way it goes beyond us. It goes down , makes a cell signal and then it says buy signal. After a few days after a few candles and is dis a by yes this is up by but within that next scandal it's a. See now why on earth it is just doing what it is doing right here. And these things sell right here and say Right. Right now this is something that is part of the game plan. Now it's said by Eric 1:53 22 settle here and said by Eric 1:53 will.

So basically from 22 to 0 4 it saved you 20 St. within these two buys. However from one for getting 22 you sold it at 150 to 87. That's approximately 13 25-35 cent loss. But this is what I call part of. You cannot ignore it. So you lost 35 things by buying here, selling here and buying here again. And once you bought it then if he moved up up up up up and said sell right to right 153 94. Now the thing to note is you want 1:52 that is full. That's a decent profit if you lost 30 -35 cents. So you're still sixty five cents in profit and there's good news that cross-compiling goes on top here. It was crossing on the low side when it went to the price crossing the building on the west side. Then I gave the stage to the risk more when it crosses to build up the price crosses the building bearing on top.

I used to risk my profile. This is simple. If the price is crossing the building going on top then this means buyers aren't happy if the price of crossing the go bang on the bottom means buyers are not. So if you like trading in it, that's far more risky if you are not trading in it. That's far more beneficial. It's up to you but I know the risk profile. Now right here CSL is sell sell sell but once it is bought again there is a higher chance it will give you that X-Gene good profit because most players are not creating fraud like this market. This whole market is not being treated by Wall Street as they wait for the sign of crossing up and once it falls in the next buy is like they're buying like deer and stuff they enter only when it's stock.

So now they know that there is a higher money making charge here. The price was crossing below doubling back. So there was a higher cost using cots right here. It is a higher moneymaking chance dots like the two phases of the. You have to understand as a day trader there are some days where you want to enter the market you simply can't because you know that the risk is far higher to make money. The risk here is far lower. What I mean to say is it's easier to make when you. There isn't much risk by care. It's double what the market is here. Risk is there but if it is let's say 10 percent here then it's 20-30 percent. All we're all here because the price knows that there's a bang. It may not cost you here.

Once you bought it the price knew that there was a cop bad. This highest moment was 155 150 455 and the highs when nobody was 154. Eighty five 86. That's only a thirty cent difference between the high and the top. Back in the day, there wasn't that much money to be made. But here there is. So if you bought at 155 28 why 55 28 you would be making money easier because that's how the scheme works. The price for oil and you would have lost money right here. 1:54 62 but that's part of the game. The trend is up. How do you know that they're right? The red line is pointing up here. Whatever red line was not pointing up at was point to ignore. So although you sold at 150 for an extra price 154 1:54.

So it's a 150 462 66 cent loss. Now if you remember we made a 66 cent profit here. It's a loss so we are still no profit no loss. Radke when the price falls, Andrei says goodbye. No right here is it. Yep 1 55 45. Joe Biden would know the red line is pointing up. So did the easier charge to make money and here Excel when you GOP 584. This falls one full to 45 so you still need a 40 percent profit. To sell. And here again it is to buy once the price crosses the blink about on top. It's by 150 630 and comes slower. That's a total loss. And here is it to buy. Yep it is. So you're buying one fifty six forty seven here and you are losing the 20th century. That's a 50 cent loss. Now you might be thinking that the plan is not working here but you're wrong because basically again the game plan remains the same. This will double talk and after that the cops are getting low.

So once the tops are getting the word then that's not a good bull run. But as long as the prices of both the lower band of toppling the bad then it means that there is a higher chance of a good trade coming around. And if you remember the previous chapters I have, almost all you do is one go create deck wipes out all those bad trades that are in the game. So you lost 30 cents here 20 Santerre approximately 50-60 cents on Rosh. And this looks to be that good Krake dislocated reboarded here at 150 670. It's currently $2 up. And here is the crossover to Lord's. You lost 60 to your $141 4 percent profit. Now this is what I call happens in 30 minutes Jacques in a 30 minute charge. There will be many many many trades all these trades one to three four five six.

All D6 take made you a 60 second loss all six straight. And this one trade bought here at 1:56 only three. That's a $2 profit huge this is what the trading plan goes for. It gives you the X-Gene painful experience of all the straight but you want to try this. It gives you an exceptional profit. That's what the game plan is. That is what the Toti means: do you have to take many Krake? If you look at it, the state has walked from December till 14 December. That's what seven eight days a week the full week. You never made money, you lost 60 percent at the end of the last 60. But right here you made two dorks within one trade and the price falls falls falls falls faults and this is the crossover again at 150 777.

So you're buying again at one fifty seven seventy seven 777 minus. Let's see what happens next. The price goes straight. Let's move this and it is like shorting. So there is a smaller chance of making money but we think the newer cell is right to sell. It is flat. Now you bought it here at 150 777. This is one of the chunky ones and it's a cell. So you lost 20 cents a day. Now you would have made $1 or 40 cents in your pocket. So now

$1 20 cent net profit. Now you might ask if a dist looks not good but this is what a 30 minute trading is. You have to create again and again and again expecting that one profitable trade to wipe all your losses out and then that $1 20 cent profit net profit acts as your game plan as your problem solver. Because in that trading on the 30 minute talk you will be having all these issues that I am just chewing you torch not something that is extraordinary.

It's something that is part of the training plan. And this can also happen. Just look at it you bought it here expecting the price to be from 57 34 and it opens lower at quantum physics 46 as you remember I told you to put a stop loss and then you wake up and it's such a gap below all the openness below all the lows. The middle though was just one thing that it does that lower the lowest even lower than these. I always sell because in this kind of situation there's something definitely wrong. And we don't know what that is. So you sell on the open even though the price can come back up. But there are some certain routes to route sales if you're wrong. Run for that or you don't wait for what has happened.

You just see it is the opening step with such a force 30 gap below doubling off and now when you are buying here you had a huge like back up plan. We had a huge gap between the building of the bank so the risk was reduced but it has suddenly opened. So you have to get out where you are again. So you won't have this kind of risk. Why? Because if you would have bought it at 157 deadfall then the next day you would have sold at 55 cents profit. Because these are the days and so we won't be waiting for the next day you'll be buying the next day or the day trader you sell before that tells you would be selling you and just opened one to me like affecting you but don't buy the tech open. And some of you have but it didn't sell because this kind of thing looked like it was never good. But Nobunaga means bad trading. And that's exactly what happened.

Now it's again that I would like to follow my plan and buy one 56 53 and the price moves up up up. But within the building of my feet it goes to the like why are and is it to sell. Nope nope nope. It opens higher but just look at it open and closed below the building. So it's down to you. There is something wrong now. If you act like you saw it on the day here you would get here at one 56 53 and total here at 156 54. So it's a flat trade within the day. Next day it opens higher above the building and that's good news right. Yes. But you have to remember if it is opening up both troubling about the Vache I always tell my student wait see what good does that take. Moosehide by 10 percent 20 percent. Let it move. Reason because it can move lower as well.

To is opening higher then and in fact is opening higher than doubling the band then waiting for the close. If it is happening in the blink of an eye then wait for the close don't buy it right then and there. If you have bought it, sell it. Just look at the chart and sell it within the first 10 seconds. It should not have come back down if it did. This decade has seen these issues and that's exactly what's happening. Or it should not have come back down. That's what the game plan is. I'm telling you a complete game plan but I'm telling you the loophole because all plants come but one size fits all. So what do do if things don't act as they should. Now it opened higher so it should have closed above troubling about it now would it.

It came back within the building about what I called the back. Once it does get out. Reason. OK. Let's presume you're wrong here. The price will move higher. What will happen is you will lose 30 -50 -60 cents or a dollar. Let it be known that trade. It doesn't matter. The question is you always have to trade using your mind and the plan because you want to get all the straight you still in that profit. We haven't lost anything. They're still net profit because this loss was not ours because at that daytrader you would have existed on this close before this close. So there is no loss for you to go public but he told you that don't buy on the open although you always buy on the open but if it opens it up. Don't buy. Wait hold right here. It opened her gawped but we won't be buying it. You'd be waiting for the coach to be sure that you are on the right track.

Chapter 7

Hi guys today you will discuss a five minute chart on the couch Q-Q power share ETF. Now it follows the Nasdaq index. We know this is one of the best because it follows one of the best stock exchange index and Daxter reasons. You have to pick one of the best stocks, an ETF or anything, for trading my plan. Now you may ask why and what is the specific reason. Now you can use a bad stock. The plan will still work but it's a bad stock that works from ten to twelve dollars. Then that's only a 20 percent difference. The plan will tell you to buy we to sell the windows 20 percent difference. So your profitability will be extremely low. But if you buy a good stock like Google and it goes from 400 to $800 and you made a 100 percent gain and the same plan would work on the one it was ending but your account will be plus by 100 percent 80 percent at a higher profit and if you're getting a backstop then your contract be up by 20 percent.

Today is like a four times difference between two stocks that have the same plan and work on both. It could be giving you the same kind of take note like your profitability would be extremely different between these two stocks the same way they didn't the IDF. If you're using a good ETF you'll make more money if you choose all these stocks. The ATF might be down by 10 percent for 2017. It might be down by 20 percent to 50 percent. So you won't be able to make money. The plan will save you those 50 Cent when you put in for but are you trying to save yourself from the fall. No. You're creating for the money. So the reason is to use stock Forex ETF wisely because the plan can only give you money from what those stocks or for X or ETF gains in itself if it gains 300 percent.

The plan will give you a good profit if it will gain 15 percent. Then the plan profitability of your own to be used at the same cost at the same ratio. It cannot increase if just talking is increasing 15 percent the plan can give you a 50 percent gain. That's common sense. That's the real thing. Now let's go on to trade five minute charts, you time to notice as we have already discussed then ever and I speak more than ever. The CD is absolute spiked pain. It makes the stock a good target to put his hands in because usually it's at the lowest point when it has fallen too much. And as you can see right here to buy things. So you can buy but it does by means that the first target is to start pulling back. You cannot expect to rise from here from 1:52 killed like two hundred and eighty dollars. That's not possible after such a fall.

But it tells you that there is a higher chance and therefore you wait for it. Now if you look at what we bought at the highest point and the stock fell off it was the lowest low of the previous fall. Here now it is because of panic for no reason. If it crosses below 10 is sequential planning. If the price crosses below the billing and Danny gets a cause of panic. It's simple. It was getting a buy signal and a major player to the buying. So to make sure that the stock or ETF fell to the lowest level and in this fall everyone was obliged to pick plex the big fish. There were all buyers here and that's why it was falling because they were making sure that it could fall. And now the retail investor panic because many of the retail investors had bought it somewhere or higher.

So once it crosses with such a velocity there are equal rights for them. And once again and it was falling so they all would have panicked and started to sell. Now to the moment in time where in that room was the community you will hear from one of the most dangerous rumors of all. He's going to make sure that people panic. And so now it is five o'clock. So the industry might not be working on the lowest level of five minutes but the concept is the same thing that you are seeing this bartering happens in all levels from daily monthly weekly to even quarterly. And I've even seen this same kind of level on your lead levels as well. Now most of you might not see it because the data provided by these companies are limited to 1972.

So that's only 15 years old, approximately 50 years. So there's not enough data backed. You might catch a glimpse of the fall like this so it takes eight to 10 years for the stock to fall to the bottom and then rise up to simple techniques like it works on each and every level. Now under all the rumors that are floating the market will be true on the level. Rumors floating in the market at this moment in time will be mostly false. It's the time frame as well that decides which thing is correct and which thing is dark now. I think in TV markets here at 150 to 40 so let's see how a trade goes. So here we go 150 to 40 Teeka price moved up above to up and now you can expect the higher highs and the price moves up up up down. Down again up up up down now now that's the thing that I call stopping or it was rising up stopped.

His first stop was the little one because this provided some one major big fish out of the stock on a five minute basis. And the retail investors pushed it higher by buying and then again selling and is it a sell. Nope this is a sale. So you would have sold it here at home in 52 40. Now you want it to act on in 50 to 40. So hanging 50 40 means a dollar a gain on a five minute chart. That's huge within the day. If you're trading a thousand a year then you have made a thousand dollar profit and you had a plan. You're not trading blindly. You had a simple plan. Just buy and sell and buy and. And now sell. So you stay out of the stock and wait for the crossover again. And that to cross or 155 34. Now if you look at it it's at the highest point near doubling of that now just dangerous. But I would still stick my guns with it. Reason is first of all I have profit in my pocket so I can risk it right here.

Second, the price was falling. Right. And this was the first time it crossed the building about an hour ago. So I can predict that from the fall there will be the high tech rise higher as it is falling. If it was not previously falling then this wouldn't have been like increasing our risk. But if you have money in your pocket then you can trade it and move higher and higher and boom it's gone now. If you focus on it you'll gain me a good amount of money. But right here there it's like I can say there is a catch. That is the date and in between. So you have to square it off right here on this date. But the question is you brought it 855 24 and sold it later turning 56 Dan to 75 cent profit the next day.

Openhearted. Two hundred and fifty sounds telling. And you look at it for 48. So that's a 20 cent loss. So again you made a 50 cent profit in this trade even though you had to get it off right here and bite at an extremely high price even then you made a good amount of money. Now if you remember I told you in the pit was like you're dead. If the price crosses the line like it opens higher then that's a dangerous sign. Yes it is. But only when the price is here and it opens higher up of the building about because the building up and it's contracting. So there's a higher chance that the price will come back in. But this thing doesn't exist because this is a completely different scenario. This opening higher and deeper exemplary discussed it opened higher So always remember the opening higher and different in terms of time means different things.

Please please please. Jim Abath because in trading not all apples are the same frenching it's different. If the billing advantage contracts and it opens higher and then like building a ban then you have to pay for the clothing. If it closes on pulling abide by it if it doesn't and comes back in that's a dangerous thing it might fall below you know like it might fall you get the lowest billing go back by cranking it had already cost to pulling it back. So it was in the Polish dot this opening hire was not considered a bad thing. This was configured on one because it's already bullish. So people are already expecting the price to go higher. So it's opening higher is a good thing. But right here big fish are not expecting the price to grow higher.

So if it is opening higher than a big face just trying to put the like his stock He's holding on to you. So don't fall into the trap if it opens higher. Very close at 155 34 to open that clunker six of one percent. So if it opens higher than the building again that's something of a problem. Example right here that's a huge gap if the gap was there. Once the price was inside the building abandoned the building and contracting then it was a dangerous sign. But the Bollinger Band is expanding and it's not contracting. So the opening is not that bad although it may have knocked me money by buying on the open selling under-class. But the point is understanding different stuff.

Now you have not made the money Stelvio ended at 50 cent profit. Brilliant. Even with that kind of risk of opening are now at fault for at fault for fault. And is it crossing the building a bank? Nope. Is it costing them health? Nope. So we still wait. Is it crossing right now? Nope it's just crossing right now. Nope context not even crossing now. So that kind of stuff but you wait, wait and wait. And you can walk by. You'll have to wait. The price is playing with you now saying by my kid at 150 893 so you can buy. But now I would suggest you could be more vigilant but stop loss of reason. You have seen many like play cards till now and you'll be seeing more chapters. Now all those chapters. How many times have you found this kind of stuff? I would say never.

It's like one in a hundred times when the MSCE isn't really Krasik. So if something is doing such a strange thing then that's a sign of a problem. So put a stop loss on the low low of descanted areas on this slowest go of the cleaned up area below the red line. It's up to you but don't place a stop loss on this kind of stuff and check their methods each and every day because it looks to be extremely dangerous to me. So I will be vigilant but I will keep on buying. I will wait for the crossover if it does not dak the extreme lowest point yes. It goes up to the extreme lowest point and boom the crossover has happened. And you said if you look at it you never made good money here.

You bought it at Winterfield 90 TESOL it at one of the 894 1 profit then a profit but that couldn't still be a bad trade when you were not sure your neighbor lost money and the fault. Faults fault fault. Just look at it when you fall off but don't go below the building. Nope that's a pretty exciting time because if it is doing something like less than that presents booms and birds fighting and fighting can cost you a good amount of money but it never went below the pulling away virtually present got the boot one ducking even though the price fell off. Now why would the price fall off when the boot opens? Because basically this is what I call the way out. Now usually if you see that the other side is selling X amount of stock X amount of EDF then you make sure that the price goes down and you buy their TGF from that guy.

Then you also notice two different means that if the person selling on thinks that is he has bought it or he's like chalk sort if he's if he's caulk sold then you make the price run up extremely fast and keep up with Shock's seller. But if he has it then you know that OK. Let the price fall a bit so that you can buy at a lower rate from that guy. But you don't make sure that the price falls further down to that. The shock comes into this is like a delicate balance when you let the shocks stay away and buy it from a seller because of the short sellers coming in. Then you have to fight on to Frank Casler and the short term and short sellers are hard to tackle.

Damfool you're trying to make sure that the price falls but doesn't fall. Extremes like below the bank level. So you keep on buying the stock or ETF as well rather than growing it like Blewett because 10 major shocks can come in and you have to put in more money to handle that stock or that ETF and usually hedge funds have limited use sorted now in Congress voters. I don't mean that they have a limited amount of money. Basically they are creating different dogs and different ETF at the same time so they have to manage them all so they don't want to create different levels of problems. They want to keep whatever it is safe as safe and deflect as you can. It remained within the building of banks.

So some major player sir and some major player bought from him and now it's moving up. Just giving you a bicycle the right one fifty nine twenty one. So let's entr'acte 150 21. Let's see what happens next. And it says sell within a few days or so within a few five minutes. That right here it's 1:58 81. So 1:58 81 minus means 14st loss and the price has gone lower. You stay out. And then within a few candles it again says by strange fact you buy. Now why would this happen. This is what I call shaking their tree. It means that when you're buying and you seed more and more retail investors like coming in front of you then you shake the tree you sell a big creek like selling pressure a fake selling pressure and upright fights and most of the investor panic and that's where it clears it up.

Now how do you create fake selling but putting in a strong sell order. Say a hundred thousand children being told that economists invest by buying 100 500 stock panic but that 200000 cheers and there was short because once you play it immediately it's taking your place of 500 years talkshow. In fact I think and then you move deck 500 and suddenly you place another 500 stock. So basically that hundred thousand dollar stock €100000 was told I don't know what's on the screen but didn't really get executed yet someone maybe you could just buy them out but they cannot buy it. We didn't make it. So a few thousand shares can be sold by the major investor but the concept is just to create a panic signal to show all the cheers. And it's like putting a thousand or a hundred shares in front of it.

So they should pick fighting power but then they would exit it and you are the investor panic and that's what happened to you. But ask for a plan B. Panic. Even We know that this is a fake panic. Still you panic. Reason because you don't want to make sure that you go against your plan and see things can go wrong extremely fast. And once they do you don't want to get caught in them. So the best way is to follow the plan. Even though it is at Sometimes it's a fake signal and you yourself know what you follow your plan so that in times in bad times you don't fall into the trap of not following a plan. Now it's again think 1:59 to a full so let's see how it goes next. Will it fall down? Or will it go up and it's an extreme level you'd get here. So any time you excel. No.

Yep now Excel again you're losing money again. Now this is a cause of concern. Always remember that this is a cause of concern because once like doing Westbrook and shaking the tree but not twice. It's a I think loss industry Ditto for making it big. It shows that it was low and now selling but we still follow our plan. And it again says by right now at 73. See again by now as a five minute chart. So these things can happen. The shaking can happen to my two part timers and you have to lose money. An extremely short period of time now five Murchadh are used by day traders and headphones don't like to create day to day trading but it doesn't mean that the shaking Latrice is happening on the day trader level as well. It could be a put like a stock hedge fund buying an ETF in the long run.

So they are shaking the tree for the long run. They might shake it for a day and you can have this kind of Kirkus but usually on the pie chart it's maximum two or three times if it comes a third time. I would get out of the stock today or if not for the day. Then he went for a rally for want after the third attempt. Now you are buying the third attempt if despite them feels like a caution trying to stay away. But usually the target never fails. But now it looks to be feeling Yep it date fill one trophy 9:24. So you lost 50 Cent on Friday 24 49 cents. Thanks to your last dollar. You made $1 50 cent profit. So now you're 50 cent plus and on the third attempt. As I told you the price just fell off and it's you and at times right below the bling upon a bad signal an extremely bad signal now it saves by right.

I wonder if that 82 you can buy. But my concept is this is telling you that there is something wrong. Now what do I mean by wrong. Let me make it a big picture. It fell off. This was the place where I told you this is the wrong movement. Then it fell off. And again this is the same picture although this was not a picture and it's not that kept. But again I think it's a sign of it could have crossed up just not crossing up to tell you there is an immediate problem. And this is how you begin to pick up one strong index stock or Forex our ETF because these are the signs that help you understand there's something definitely wrong. And that's how you begin to be concerned. Thank you.

Chapter 8

Hi guys today we will discuss Amazon Dot com. This is a brilliant start. And that's the reason I selected it to train you on a good stock now. Always remember any stock. I mean any stock that you hear the name again and again in your friend list in your colleagues list like they are discussing that company and in Bloomberg or CNN if you're hearing the company name again and again good or bad that means that companies are bound to make a good investment. It will make huge huge sums of money. Now this is one of the best cut criteria to pick a stock. The reason. See, let me explain to you the psychological thing.

If you see an ad of any product 10 times then once you go into the shop and you see two different products one for which you have seen the ad and one for which you'll see not at and like no at Daniel consider the add one although they are made by the same company and same product and everything is same then you you will pick that up even though on the news you might have heard good and bad news now by bad news. I don't mean exceptionally bad news but bad news I mean some bad news like exporter really not good and things like that because basically those bad news are created to make sure that you really are dealing with her.

Don't jump in because a major investor knows that it's a good company. Then comes the confirmation indicator. Now I have to for our chalk right here and zoom back till the date I can have and this is to like last get Hadayet. I have now the first thing in this trading and my CD trading is divergence. Now if I show you the price here, sorry. Here is at 5:57 36. And on this end it's 580. So the price is higher right. If we consider this high then when it's higher they make just a crying line from these high till this high. Then the trend line is higher. But if I just zoom onto a CD and I make a trend line from this high till this I then explore more than ever this is a bad signal. Now I'm telling you that Amazon is a good stock but right here I'm telling you to get out. That's what the trading plan is the trading plan because things that are not good enough and it tells you to get out or get in.

And if you look at it, the stock did fall off. Now right here I've stopped. I'm not going for it because I want to teach you a second tool. This pulls up and if you look at the building up and all the rest act as a stopping point of the prices falling then the lowest point of the building acts as a support because if it falls further down then it will go below the building of an anvil move for the lower. So this is a major support now. Usually in a bull stock from here it will jump back up and just look at it from here. It opened higher and is like now on a good note I'd move higher higher higher higher.

But if you look at the Ballingall back story MSCE it keeps on falling. It's kind of like it's going down down down. So this is like two different ways to go to number one and Methodism tells you what is happening. If the price is bullish or bearish Now more on now and UCD here is telling us bearish but right here belong again it tells us what the price is doing. If the prices within the band then it's unlikely to make you a huge profit. It will just move within it if it moves higher than the billing upon above or lower than it will usually follow the trend if it is lower than it will follow that trend down. If it is higher then it will follow that trend up. Now MECC if you look at it it's British.

Now if it is Baelish you and I might consider the next charge. Now Oldershaw itself is not a bad thing but if you look at the blink of an eye the price hasn't crossed lower the price right here. The low is 540 88. But like right here the loan is 5:55 So the low they're higher but the MLC continues to go lower right here the Methodius on the two minute click. We checked 5.1 and right here the lowest point was five point ninety six like going down. See that's not a good thing. If I move a bit more damage Siddiq continues to go lower. Now I always remember the highest and lowest points of Fehmi MSCE. Really important if it's breaking this low point then it's an exceptionally bad thing.

But you don't jump into the stock just on damaske. Look at doubling up now the pulling off and on the flipside is making sure that the price doesn't go below doubling of it. Now it's going lower, doubling up and has started to move down. Harold Ford moving up to just a bad signal. But the real bad thing happens when the price goes below the UP. Right now it's not gone below it saying that the trend is going down. And that's a bad thing. But it's not saying that the acceleration in fall is coming. Now how did we know that the stock was not good. First it was divergence and the second bad thing was once it broke so right here on 5:56 Amazon was an extremely bad investment and it continues to go lower.

Now it's jumping back up and up. Now the thing to note is it never went below the building again. Yes it did hit it and tried to change the train. But now it's moving up again. Now is the Oremus really saying by no it's gaining a very from now right here. This is what I call the cross or now just to show you if I make it big. These are the numbers shown here. Three numbers. If I put my mouse right here it's showing that first of all let me put it here. Now the blue line is lower and the red line is higher. Whenever this happens then the first number will be in minus minus represents Sal. Always remember the first number here that represents minus. It means to sell the next number is the blue line number wherever it is trading.

And the third number is the red line number which is the moving average of the blue line that tells you the red line number. But remember the first number that it's in minus. It does sell. And once it is right here it tells me this is the number one thing. So it told us to buy right here at 560 963. Let me put it in I couldn't for a minute right here it Kibei signal. OK. Now the thing to note as I want to make sure that you know all the problems. The thing to note is always remember as long as the price stays within the billing of and that's a good sign you can do it. And Missy was telling us that it's a bad stock and the price was not going anywhere. But the CD was falling off. So that means that you can sell but you can ShoreTel Now Mo.

Number two whenever the price lake stays there and makes Double-O example the first low, this is the second low and comes back up. That's a great pull sign. Always remember if this is the Brillion Boatright but don't buy it. They wait because the point is not to lose money. Making money is the easiest part. It will automatically come. I look at it. The price rose up and now it's going down. Why? Because we are currently locked in the building of the building that I ended up telling us there go buy signal was not that bad. It means we are on the right track. But the price hasn't crossed it. Therefore it's a bye moment but not a superbike moment. Now there are two moments. One is a buy , one is a super buy and the same big one sells.

Example you could have sold it right here on MSCE crossed the red line down right here. That was a salting of 570 sounds with the cell signal. Right. But if only a cell , not a supercell, would have come in once the price would have gone below the baby. Now it is but it stuck. It moves higher and nearer to the building back number one. Number two as you can see the building is rising this high is like this rising price. It's brilliant. It means the polish. Now if you know what candlestick is then candlestick itself is telling us that it gets a bullish signal. If you don't know then you can learn from your Dammy and I have a Book in that too. Now if you look at this price this size tells us that it's a super power by now for Super by I will be selecting items up and for supercell Oliver selecting items John. Now right here it's a thumbs up.

Now if you look at it the price goes higher higher now it drops it's dropping. See that's a bad thing. But we will stick to our guns. We'll stick to your guns and right at the last moment. It goes below. And if he goes below once it does that sell. But remember one thing and that's right. Like a really important thing now, the remembering thing is looking at the MATV now the MSCE drops the price but destroys the Gunda line to support. Just look at it right here to support the next day it opened higher and it's moving higher now right here in the open. His own 0 6 underclothes was fired at 14. So it's down the next week and opened at 588 which is higher than the open close here. Why? Because this red line is bringing support now it's moving up.

Right. But has it crossed the red line? No. So be vigilant. But it's a bold sign. Now it moves up a notch dropping if I just make it big. Just look at this and just drop had this woman get six point eight seven. And this low is seven point five. So it's breaking the previous two. Whenever this happens it's a bad thing. And from here Friday night you five. I am expecting 570 to 20 doors down simply. Nothing extraordinary and it drops but just look at it. The red line continues to support it. Now number two thing is now a shock to sell a stock based on the MSEE crossover all with for the embassy to break the previous low. And the price to be nearer are below the billing and lordling don't shock sell.

Before I look at it, that's where I also call it the Kenyan track. Now remember ads were discussed right here the top guys the same thing happens right here. The laws as the laws move higher. It means the price is moving higher. But we will wait for the crossover. And right it's the crossover and it will run its full sea. So it's like buy and super buy on the same day on the theme for our canon. Now this is the day trading Book in day trading when you see these kinds of two good signals. Boom it's up by now. 6:13 is the moment and just look at it. Within a few days it went to 6:23. That's a $10 profit without doing anything. And it moves higher and higher. Now this is a bad kind of stake moment when the price eats the previous day's giant bad thing. But if I just show you right here this is what I call the bore down on the long term.

What is the bull run? First of all the price never crossed below zero. Now this is the zero mark and see the real Mark. The price should not be below zero below zero means there is no trust in the stock. It won't make you more money. Now above zero means it's a good long run. So the test is on the buy if it is below zero then the test is on the sell. This is a very interesting learning point. The third point is this kind of thing. Now the highs are getting higher the Whenever this happens. It means that in the longer run you should be expecting the price to rise. And if I move further the price is not going anywhere. Now once the MSEE broke doing every red line and had a crossover right here. It was a cell signal. You would have sold it to him and it made me pick it up.

Yep right here. And it's saying that it will drop from there till this moment. Approximately $600 now currently 670. Now why do we believe it's going lower and why her trailer went lower. The reason being the red line right. It never crossed the red line on the lower side. Right here it is crossing on the lower side. And the price goes straight straight drops drops and now it is super sell. It's below the red line. Now how can we know it has to be pushed before time. That's the number one question and the answer lies if we just remove death. And if you see my doctor line right here. Once the MECC broke the previous lower IQ disproofs low as 5:56 this is 5:24 if I zoom out then let me bring it supercell right here.

This is the super cell. If you look at it once the MTD broke the previous low it was like hell breaks loose. And once the price fell below the billing going to supercell. And if you look for the price is not acting like the price goes below and goes up. Now you might ask how it helped. It's super confusing. The price went lower and I said supercell and it went higher. Now doctor I tell you another golden rule. Now once it broke this moment which was this day 6:16 it went lower to see a little too right. But just look at it. This report is broken. This report comes in and zero is considered to be far more important than other supports. And it came back to this lowest point was the 0.6 line it was at the lowest point number two.

So whenever you break a low then it goes to the second floor from if it broke this low. Then it was Gilda's law. So it's like bull signal number one. Number two once it broke it and the price went lower and certainly opened higher and went lower. This is not a good sign. It's opening higher. Always remember in a fall that opening high should never be above the highest point of the for example this high point it made in your high. Why on earth is it making a new high? It should be breaking the lows not making when you're high and it's made in your. You went on this fall. It never crossed. Lor it should have. Now it doesn't. Now it's saying buyer I care. But on the CD is it a buy.

No. So you will wait and try to buy. Now this is a day trading Book. In a day trading you'll have many many. Now for just sure you re Borchert hair at 569 and sold it here at 5. Now from a day to or prospective that's so NJT 19:24 our profit 6 12 18 24 that's a 4 percent profit Vitt then the intraday period. If you look at it right here we bought it at 6:13 29 and we sold it here at 6:31. That's again $18 profit, a huge 2 percent profit and now it's a gain thing by letting me get Dyken for you. Wait a minute right here. Again things buy and the price moves higher higher higher. Now if I just focus on the MSCE then it has crossed a pretty high and that means that the second Hydes here fate will be getting the second high.

Now the MF Hedy's dropping and tells you to sell right here. So if you would have it here at 6:59 you would have sold it at 665 again and to Ford our profit although it's not a big profit point but the point is it's a brilliant profit. It's a brilliant profit because if you look at the order internally, creating is profitable and I'll be discussing different clocks one hour Lee and others so that you can understand if you want to create sharper ones like Chuck's example one hour and below 20 when this plan works. But the point is you have to first learn ego. You have to understand what each and every perspective tells you. Now right here retreated one two three three traits and all are profitable on day to day level.

Now if you have created inter-relate well or if your friends are afraid they will tell you it's not that much easy but right here I've just shown you a normal tank and it has worked on each and every time. That's the power of a plan. Now in the next chapter your list goes to hourly chalk so that you can understand how an hourly chart can make money and easy money. But always remember the lesson of the chart, the letter the money now right here. I showed you up for two. Like one to four percent profit. But on the hourly charge the profit percentage will start two degrees but it will stay profitable. The point of view is to stop the losses and that's where building a bank comes in. And in the next chapter I will discuss how. Thank you.

Chapter 9

Hi guys today we will discuss one hour in chalk on Amazon.com. Now all these like Bies helps to know that what you're seeing are from the four hours you choked Now as you can see it's got and will move further down down. Now it's saying so we will place a signal right here. Now if I just place time I'll try Terry you can see that the first number is in a positive sign. Right. On this day at 671 80 to 60 $171 82 you'll be buying an hourly Chuck. So please remember you can not wait and take hourly charts and below charts that are called blind for trading in blind for trading you just rely on your indicator and nothing else. You can not do anything. You simply cannot do anything and that is our number one rule. Now if I just show you something.

Now if you remember the four hourly charts we report right. But if you look at the hourly chart the crossover happened right. You would have bought it at six twenty two and it went higher. See now it is a buyer I can't ever say is buying right here. We wait and the price moves higher and higher. So it's like really easy money to be made. The price goes higher higher higher and it still continues to go higher. That's the big deal. It goes higher higher higher higher higher. So you bought them here at six seven and eight you and now at $715. And what are you following only the crossover IQ. And it still continues to say by now it just started to move down. If I just you mean just look at it it has fallen.

But you will wait for it to cross over. And if you look at it for the if I just put my mouth there it's minus 0.09 89. So it's a cell signal right here at 17:14 you bought 671 few daughters to Tricare to sell 30 40 $45 at $42 profit. Huge. And this was what I call super by now in our trading. This is the moment where a call to the moment of silence always remembers this for just zoom out to show you and let me show you these are like the previous like when Mark word Colline right here was like done these four lines sorry these two lines is our four hour chart within these two lines. OK. Now if you look at it this is the first time this is the second night when it reached the second and started to go lower. That was like a signal that will drop but this drop which means from 635 you would have seen 600 orders easily.

That's a 5 percent fall. That's huge isn't it now. Right extolling the theme. Now I'm not saying this is a shock sell signal. But what I'm trying to say is this is a cell signal in a perfect setting. I told you that the market is going down now to make the market move higher on our low level things seen in debate. And how did they do that? Did that with a simple technique. Diablo's not only is he the first loads the second go and it moves higher. This is the first low, this is the second low and it moved here. This is the first low but the second law was broken and it went lower. This is Davalos' number one thing Davalos. However some of you will be thinking that right here it cross-strait up there is no Double-O.

And I'm telling you that DeLillo's present is a crane. Now wait a minute. There is a light difference that no one will teach you. That is after it crosses the peak this peak right here it crosses right here somewhere. And that's to me you teach something now on here on the first by you won't be making easy money. That's guaranteed you win right. If you were to walk right here at 6:20 for a fall, you wouldn't be able to make money. Right. If you're at a bar on the first try, food has not made you good money. But once it crossed it from here at 600 you would have gone to 6:27. That's it. The highest dollar bill's highest point is 6:37 and right here at 6:33 to that attorney your eyes are five percent huge isn't it.

Now right here we are discussing that there is no Double-O. So what do we do in that sense? Right on this fall there is no Double-O all the days to load this Double-O this Double-O but right here it is don't Double-O and that's where I call it either go for the lay cross over number one and number two the last thing off Bordeaux below the second best is crossing the side and I look at it the price of MSCE was falling. It spiked up. If you just focus on the blue number. OK. Blue is the blue line of this MECC X 1.3 for the open denying minus 1.8 for minus 2.6 minus three points down for minus 4.6 9 and now minus five point rates which draws a bit up sorry from 4.6 9 it went to four point five and then fell off 5.2 riot 515 5:41 and then it started right back up.

So it crossed this first meeting. The second week you know and then it went up. So this is the second best thing. Now right here we have bought and it's dropping so it's making a snap. You'll like this now that it's a vertical divergent scenario. Inner divergence what really happens is the first high and the second high on the hourly level is lower. Now this won't show you on though for all you know but if it does then for hours to proceed everything and if I spawn from here deals this high point here then the price has risen by the MTD has fallen. That's a bad signal. And that's exactly what happened. Now right here on this moment today right here it's doing this exact same thing the price has gone from here.

682 till 720. Right. But the MSEE has gone lower now. Whenever I say lower then things can change as well from the next day. Always remember this. It's not like a confirmation that it can change but the concept is for a change from the previous high. That is, this high is far nearer. So your risk for that looks extremely low. If it moves higher than a CD moves higher than it will cost us first and it will move higher. So this line will be finished and will be an upgrade again. But as of now it's thin behavior and if I just zoom in. The price continues to go straight. But the MSCE continues to fall. Now if I just move to chapter do you go further your price goes higher.

That is decoupling . Now you might ask what the hell is happening. The price continues to go higher but the endless CDs dropping now and when you see this get out don't get into the stock because this is exactly what happens to price drops and even crossed the lower end go back to bad stuff. Extremely bad stuff. That's never a good thing. Now we saw Dick right here at $740. Currently the price of that sounded A1 and then insidious continuously dropping dropping dropping. Now it's moving higher but dropping again now it's moving down again now it has reached zero point zero point. As I've discussed it is a good support signal but it has now dropped below zero point. As of now it's currently trading at minus 1.2 for tonight.

And if you remember the previous chapter I told you when and where the price goes below zero then the trust on the downside increases rather than the upside. When you add the MSDS above to zero the trust on the up side is increased rather than the fall. So now it's below zero. Now that's a thing that you should keep in your mind. Now if you see a buy signal MUTV crossing its red line that will be far weaker. Far lower profit to profitability will be reduced by extremely low stagnant. You won't be able to make huge sums of money even if it is below zero. This is the number one rule. Example right here cost right. If you read it here at 6:59 you would see tactics only 5. OK but if you would have bought here at the cross or 671 you would have made huge sums of money far higher than you made here. You made money here.

But this money was higher than this money. Why? Because it went from zero like below from minus it went to the bluff market right here. It was already plus it never went below zero. So the power of the higher is extremely high. Now I am talking about minus and plus about the blue line. So don't confuse the first number with the first number. Only about crossover if it goes below the red line then X minus 40 days above the red line X plus. But if the blue line itself goes below zero that's a bad thing. And now it has gone below zero. So now expect the buy signal to be the V just extremely weak the price goes straight straight down down down. And now it's crossing a fee.

That's what I call a bold sign. Remember but to buy signals will be extremely Veeck so don't x a good profit don't expect huge sums of money. Be vigilant. I'm saying it's a bicycle or 698 you do but I'm saying be vigilant. Reason. Just look at it. The price never crossed nibbling a band on top. Bad signal. If it doesn't that's not a good sign and drops drops drops drops drops drops. And if I just zoom in it's now again going below zero. Bad things are extremely bad. Now right here on this moment I always tell my students to place a stop loss either below the straight line number one or below your like cattles low. This is the number one thing now. If you place a red line and the price leks preview it rises like this.

Then your stop loss will automatically increase. You'll be increasing it every day according to the deadline and when to say sell those simplicial and cancel their cell or a stop loss order. Simple enough. But if it happens like this then your stop loss order will hit. And you will get out. And once you are out. Let's presume you boarded here right. Sorry. 698. And let's presume you please just stop loss on the right line and right on this day. I take it you are out right. It's 700. So it's an hour 's profit. The lowest 698. So let's presume we made no money and no profit. OK so we won't be jumping in to buy one more. Who will be waiting for the blue line to go lower and uncrossing higher. OK wait it drops now.

On this day it has crossed up again by signal right exactly. So we'll be buying it again. Right here. Sorry I couldn't and here is the buy signal rate rate now. But if you look at it I will restore to you on this or the first time this is the Fechner adaptable signal. But if it never crosses that high and I don't mean this high I mean. This pulling back check cross out look at it. The price is not making a good comeback. I did open higher but again excluding straight I look at this is the first load this is the second low. It's moving higher. Let me show you right here. It's a good signal. Not a bad signal but some things definitely don't actually go higher. Now what do you like?

What do I mean by saying there is something wrong. Now just look at this like her ice up on a CD. Now this is something not a I cannot explain on paper. It's something that you need to understand yourself so it's like a bit of a problematic part for me. But I'm sure that one day a few who will learn this thing will be far better than adults. So this is an important mark that is right the spike up now. Yes. If you look at. Let me bring it back to Dula they demand please. It is a tool that can give you the angle at which it grows up. Nimble 60 degree angle or 80 degree angle stuff like Doc and that can help you understand what the angle of their eyes is.

Now I cannot find a tool as of now. OK let's leave that out. But the point is to look at the angle. This is a sharper angle within a few hours. It grows extremely sharp within a few hours. It grows extremely sharp but right here even in all those hours it's not that sharp. It's extremely weak. And if you look at the price from just Double-O or from this high flier there are five after so many hours it's still only 214 215 that's only $10 again. That's not a win again because commissions a child at $5000 physics. It's not even covering commissions whenever this happens. Be vigilant and not think about selling because of selling. Always follow my train. Now if you look at it the last closing flight just to get in right here it's saying crossborder.

That's a cell signal. So sell it. But remember the thing. Remember this moment. This is the moment for you. And what do I mean by that? Let me tell you first lick me please. I can be sorry for the misplacement. I didn't place them all you didn't want to buy. This is the cell. But it's not to my liking. So I'm not DECT much happy. But my point is when you see this kind of a situation and on the rise up from zero that's a bad thing. It's a present extremely bad law coming up. And now it's cell phone duty. The price rose backfire. See now this will always happen or now the car. Now this is a thing that you and I cannot ignore. Wait a minute. Let me place it correctly right here it is. But let me place it. Right.

Now it told us to sell. Right. But on the next day it crossed the Amasia. So always buy it. But when and where you are buying on the lake range up an example right here. So I'll just leave it with a stop loss example on the low of the scanner, a stop loss below the straight line. Now once more the price now from 780 has gone to 725. Not that much of a higher spike but if you look at the empty seats again not fixed not on a higher angle. It's stopping at every moment. Now this is the thing where I call major listeth getting out of the market. This is the deal dead sign that major investors are moving out and you as a small investor should be vigilant now. This is the thing and this represents a huge fall coming up as well.

But just look at the camera's slow 673 and its high 720. This is a product that people got out and grabbed the eagle investor that is you. Now how could we know that this follows coming to reason? Or the answer is this lot when it broke this low radio right here it was a complete signal that a price can have this thing. Now I always remember when I read the MSCE breaks its previous lows then you can see terrible things like this extreme falls extreme things. And on the lower side if it causes the highs previous highs then you will see good things happening. Example extreme But this represents trading fun. This represents the huge fight going on between balls and beards. Now I look at it.

It fell off and then came back up. Why? Because once it broke the previous low then this fall could have happened and grasping the leveraged Byars so the leverage started to like sell and then some intelligent investor came up and bought it again. Now if the price of above doubles a ban then he could present the chances of going lower. It's extremely rare. There is a roulette market and that rule is that this low will be touched either today like within a few days or within a few weeks or within a few months but it usually comes back to hit a low. He said that it will be Embleton. Now if you do and we sell it on the MSCE cross or wait a minute Reika that's a minus. So now VSL.

Now you might ask should we buy it here. Yes you could but be vigilant and always place a stop loss below the red line that G.R. like a Life-Saving line. You Bodek here. And within a few days we saw it. So this is the last trade right. We didn't two days within two hours we sort and the price is not looking good to me. So the embassy is not looking good to me and the pricing would not look good to me why. Because if I just do I hope now I have zoomed out and if I just place a line on the line right on this high What do you see the price is stuck in between that moment. It's not going anywhere. Neither high nor lower. That's not a good thing. That represents someone big who is selling. Now MEAC is a brilliant tool to gather that information and place your trade always according to him.

Why would you and let's presume you didn't pick that up. It's a good thing or bad. Still in this shorter moment of time when I'm saying I myself as confused we want to hear sound reifies sold here at 7:30 that's an $8 profit. One percent profit we bought here. So in 18 and slicked down 20 do we get to $4 a profit. That's even affording our profit that's a half a percent profit from this moment. Right. You lost me. That's the first time around 28. This low is sound 22:6 lost 1 percent loss. But the concept is you are all within profit you make money here as well here as well.

That's up one and a half percent profit to trade and you lost 1 percent. So on the net basis you're still half a percent in profit at the end of the MEAC. It always saves you from the hassle. It always keeps you in profit. However you'll be trading far higher density trading. But Dax thought a treatment is about now in the next chapter we will discuss and chalk that would be shorter. DM So that I can help you explain how to trade you one charge at home because right now we're discussing one hour and the next will be extremely short chalk. So stay with me and increase your knowledge. Thank you.

Chapter 10

Hi guys today you will discuss Amazon Dot Com on 15 minute jocks. So it's really fast. I'm out of trading outside trading where I always tell my student you should not take yes you heard it correctly. I'm saying don't take it because the training is so fast that if you were like pink and really took a minute on thinking then in that dance price can move from you and you can use the girls in touch because 15 minutes trading five minutes training 30 minutes trading. It's something you cannot even invest one minute of thinking about. If you go beyond that let's say our game plan 10 you can take a minute to think. But if you go on to win it you are doomed to fail. Therefore remember as you move toward the lesser trading pattern you don't take and create if you will think you will lose money.

Now if you come to a trading plan I need to show you something. And this is what I call the go down thing. This is a trading pattern where most traders don't like a CD and you have this MSCE alone. They simply don't understand. And then boom is money. Now I was telling my Kodo when I made an error and when thinking went up, down came back up to the second highest. So usually after the second night it falls off and goes lower. Right. But here you can see it took the support and started to like it moved beyond the red line right here. Now when it does taste that details this is first and second. And this is first of all second low first confusing you so much like shock sell or you should buy. Both are not conforming.

When this happens, I put a box on a chart . For example , I'm putting a horizontal line on a desktop point and on this talking point like me, pick it up again. Right here now I put a light line and that boot in there fighting and when it's burning. So how will you know to make a crate and I look at it. This car is like a box for just going out a bit. Yeah. As you can see in this box, what you see is really tough fighting. And if you remember the building here now the newer machine is confusing and it's fighting on its own to stay on the sidelines and only trade once the price is tumbling for that reason. Because once the fighting stocks on a CD you mostly back fighting stocks one but once the price is within the building go back and then put the bank contract example right the left between the two.

Let me make a line to show you a credit line from Stop point to all this broken plank off paying the bank. Now I'm not picking anything else. I've just picked it up and the bottom and if I get here then to get off to building a bank is nearly half the gap has dropped to half. If I move my pin on that right it has dropped by one third extremely going lower. Not a good mark for a king. It goes beyond like it expands a bit but if you look at the bright it's not going beyond building a bank. So it tells us that even though it's expanding but not in a good shape. And that's exactly what happened. It contracted again and this time the contraction is even sharper. This is 20 percent of Rockefeller's decline in Coke less. This was a big baker. This was extremely small.

So I guarantee you that is a problem. If we move again right here you see the same thing again. It's now 10 percent of whatever this line is. So it tells you that the building was contracting and when we're building a business contracting intellectual I think it's any CD or any other tool I repeat and you go they will go dark and you want to be able to make money. And that's the reason I'm putting wooing a band on the chart because basically you have to have a backup plan if and when you do field then you move forward and you look and if you look after people who don't trust technical indicators the reason is this kind of movement once any indicator stocks in a play going up in a box they create havoc on trading plan and that Hairlock like great confuses people.

They're like "What the [REMOVED] is happening?" And Doctor your problem Tefal the solution lies in Berlin go back and if I mistake confusion stay out and wait for tippling back to price to cross-compiling. Now you might say that based on this don't eat up and hide under the gun. Yes it did but it turns lower. Bad move. Again it went higher and closed lower. Now to the back. A good move. Therefore you have to wait. You know if you remember we are in a box from Florida and if I guess you mean you are still in your book. Now this is the first day I had a big first day where the prize just crossed the building and I am putting it up and I am putting up an arrow so that I can assure that this is the bye signal.

So if two are stuck then you have Buckethead Turkey in 84. Now you have Brockett. But if you look at them a CD is still in the box. Yes, two blue lights. It's not a good sight , correct. Not a good template but if you just look at it, what's the price ? It went beyond like two buildings and it went straight up. And if I just put them in the embassy I also crossed and broke this highest line once built. Now it's moving higher now and then to a point to remember zero of a CD. Whenever you flirt with you, that's not a good plan. It almost confuses you because most headphones and big play is considered to be the holy grail. If Zeus crossed the module going by or and other kinds to consider short selling damfool that's a problem because if somebody tingles short selling and some unagi when thinking by then it means the price can go lower but the price is not going lower.

This means that someone else is buying. So it's like completely fighting on and before always we never do the war going on outside. Once the war settles and the price goes up to building a band on another building band then this gives you an insight. OK. This is happening by and therefore you can see the price rises and now it comes within the blink of an AND IF I just move to the last extended 0.1 one per move beyond this is minus two. This is the cell signal. We brought it. I will tell you this is going to mean that it's still $12. Now you might say that's extreme but it's still 1 percent gain. And remember this is a 15 minute chart. So it's 15 to 20 minutes one hour one two three four two hour one two three four three hour one two three four four hours and 30 minutes and you are out of sync within four hours. And now it's like it crashed down.

So it's moving down. And now the prices are again on the verge of moving up and that looks perfect. And you can buy and look at it pulling up and telling you a day earlier right here when tech crossed however you are going to believe you can put a stop loss on the lowest point of that day either on this low or the extreme low here. But don't trade with the stop loss reason. Reason being that the bank can move up and down. Number one. Number two is MSCE when you see this coming back it can be like the second high and drop off. So if you're trading with a stop loss look out if I could break it pretty slow. If it does, that's not a good plan. But now here you can see the price move higher. And write it move or he says minus 0.03 the first mark is the plus or minus C minus when he makes mine.

It means a cell signal when you get it. Plus it means a buy signal. So right here you would have food. Now we brought it here at 23. We sold it here at 45. That's $22 and that's twenty four five six seven eight nine ten thirty approximately three hours. That's not a bad trade. Again you have made a placenta soy that's $20 to approximately purposely million isn't it. Within 24 hours on a bad move. And if you look at it further to go sell sell sell. Now if you look at it the prices will be higher back Timothy D's moving lower. Now take notice is the price crossing or pulling a band that's an important thing even if it does then you when I tell you all this to please stop loff never to cross-state. Just like that right here it is costing up now.

Our aim is not generating the signals. Feeds Norcross who are still minus 0.2 now. Whenever this happens you can get to the buy signal. But your aim will be to stop loss and you'll be looking at the lowest point off the CD. If it was white it means it was a fake signal to always remember this and I'm familiar with it. You bought it right here at Tony takes you to the next to last left but the next day it jumped up to 76 and the high was 13. Eighty six from there 62 tax 24 not 2 percent gain. And if you look at now this is in the pocket like chapter art stuff the thing that will change your game plan. Now if you're looking at it, move up right here. Right. We bought it on this day. One ticket crossed the building line up.

That takes you to the price went up. It fell off and it moved up again. This is what I call the second high. But let fall is the plan. It drops the next day. Now on this day it is breaking the empty CD. It is the crossover. See that's minus zero point tonight right here. So that's a sell signal. Let me first place Aiken right here. You bought it at 62 and we sold it at thirteen sixty three. So it's flat trading. No problems now. Always remember the one thing in trading is if you're following my plan that I am discussing here then every day before the market closes 15 minutes or 30 minutes straight in front of the stock market and check to see what he does. He learns from it and makes a decision within the last five to 10 minutes.

That's by now right you excelled. OK. So we are told flat no profit no logic. But what do you see right? We see the first high and the second. Now if it breaks this low then that's not a good sign because then we can expect them to actually fire the Sellwood and if it falls still that level then that's not a good moment. The shift in the stock now although we've already sold. But you have to like to check the nerves of the market to understand what is happening. Now within the next fall too. OK. Let's move further. Now it has fallen even below and it has broken this low. Now when it breaks this low then the market becomes I would call it extremely rollock I got to be extremely what you need to cross the billing about on the lower end to fall off.

Now it hasn't Costic part to MSCP half. So it tells you that the market is not a good position. And what really happened. Just look at it, it did fall off but not with the same force. Now once this happens that is also a good sign. Why? Because if the polling is bad, if the embassy is breaking the flow and the price is not really that interesting This means that we're in a good stock because if it is breaking the pin was loose on day misleading and the price all to Freiler that they need to in like just fall off. Now that is good in the short sale scenario but if you're looking for a good stock to buy now you then this kind of a move doesn't follow them a CD it's continued to be exceptionally good stock because it tells you that the current emceed the big giant pool everyone to sell.

No one was willing to like chalk sell because basically short sellers are the most risk takers and if you're not jumping into that stock and they're not like taking that stock that means that stock has something great in it. It's not like just a normal back stock. Now just look at it. Oprah and he fell off all fell off and in all the respects Debt-Free made like many 15 candle's ago. It just took a support on that level and now it's pointing up. But it is a busy thing. No you stay out stay out. Now right here this is the crossover. Now the prox was important once it was within that box. Not now. So you can buy it as well but as you can see that the price is within the billing of back.

So whenever it is Fintain doubling again then be vigilant. And if you remember my previous chapters then the 20 day is for your help but it's a 15 minute chart. So be vigilant. However I did for a 20 minute line as a stop loss signal and also followed the MSCE line as a shop. Now if you look at it you're stopping at the same high. That's not a good sign. But usually I don't follow the signs at this moment because it is right here. I believe you should just follow them because they feel confused. I'm uber scared of mental blocks that really cause huge problems. Now you Southern Partisan. This is what I call the second high. Dr. Klein went up. Now it's again confusing. So we'll wait for day to day 40 just to see if it crosses town. If it does that's a cell signal and a brain cell signal because it will be first tie in second.

But if you look at no cost. It stayed in the Book. But it's extremely painful going up and now it looks to be perfect. And if you look at it you know what I've brought here is turning 65 it's just turning 20. It's not even a profitable trade. But he will sit on the sidelines and wait. Now you might ask why is the street not that much profitable. Pewsey you are seeing exceptionally good trade and that's we're building a bank that comes in and helps you understand the volatility. If you look at aid to pan here it is extremely shocking. So it tells you there is no movement and if there is no movement in price then there is no life and price and without life you cannot make money.

So it's if you look at it. You went after buying and seeing so many candidates you were just flat out no profit no loss. You just flat black flag. But if you look at the empty CD it's still not getting a cell signal. So you have to sit in it and bid it out. And right here to sell said to yourself. Now you brought it here today and 65 out sell at 2069. So it's still flat, no profit , no loss. But the concept in itself is that you follow the plan and end the trade. Black and now you look at it further to him as he falls off and moves higher again. But the first time was an exceptional moment, the best moment. That is it has crossed it has crossed to pulling back and Dafoe it tells you now it's time to party. It's time to make good money.

And this is currently trading at 13 in filled and it closes higher than doubling about if you remember. Let me just zoom out. Sure. Moment. Yep right here. This opened higher as it opened higher but it closed on all but more troubling about the toppling of the bank. Now when it does that that's not a good move but here it opened higher and close lower back up both to build back. That's a good sign. That's not a bad sign. And just look at it, it went higher. It went higher. You see the line is still crawling up and that's what tells you that you are on the right track or not. All right. On the downside. So you sell let me get to I can and we saw it right here. Now where did we talk to Kit Tony and why did we close. Cody 98. Even if we look from the 0.39 on Dec. 30 98 that's seven dollars.

That's half a percent profit, not a bad move. But then one two three four one hour one two three four two hour one two three four three hours and 15 minutes. Half a percent gain. And the best part is you're following a plan. You know what is happening. You're trading according to the plan. But two different things. It's 15 minutes so you should shop at the lake or you cannot just wait and look for prices. This kind of trading means extremely chokri, usually people who trade 50 minutes or 30 minutes or even one hour trade with computerized programs so that it automatically sells really fast. But the point is it's up to you. This is the true trading market. So if we say so just go around and sell me fast. Don't let it fall.